Highlights

GRADES K&1

Summer
Big Fun Workbook

Published by Highlights Learning • 815 Church Street • Honesdale, Pennsylvania 18431
ISBN: 978-1-68437-289-8
Mfg. 04/2020
Printed in Mattoon, IL, USA
First edition
10 9 8 7 6 5 4 3 2

For assistance in the preparation of this book, the editors would like to thank:
Vanessa Maldonado, MSEd; MS Literacy Ed. K–12; Reading/LA Consultant Cert.; K–5 Literacy Instructional Coach
Kristin Ward, MS Curriculum, Instruction, and Assessment; K–5 Mathematics Instructional Coach
Jump Start Press, Inc.

Say No to Summer Slide . . .

Your child's summer learning adventure starts here!

This book is divided into eight chapters, each designed to bridge kindergarten and first grade and give your child practice in a variety of curriculum areas all summer long.

Tips for using this book with your child:

1 Find the right time.
Whenever possible, start new activities in the morning or following a snack or meal—any time she is well fed and rested.

2 Let your child take the lead.
If your child is eager to keep going, encourage him to do so, but don't pressure him to complete a certain number of pages or even finish an activity.

3 Take it with you.
Learning can happen anywhere. Bring this book with you during your summertime travels for learn-on-the-go fun in the car, on a plane, or even in the backyard.

4 Pour on the praise.
When your child works hard on an activity, acknowledge her efforts enthusiastically. She'll love that you're excited, and she'll be happy about her efforts and actions.

5 Join the fun.
At the end of each chapter is a bonus activity, such as a recipe, craft, or science project. You can also extend the learning by playing math games—using dominoes, dice, or a deck of cards—and by encouraging your child to notice letters and words on signs at stores or when you go for a walk.

and Yes to Big Fun!

As your child journeys through the book, she can track her progress by placing stickers on the **Summer Big Fun Adventure Poster**.

Here's how:

1. Remove the poster from the back of the book and unfold it. Hang it up or place it on a flat surface.
2. To advance along the path, your child will complete the activities in a chapter of the book.
3. When your child has completed a chapter, he will place that chapter's sticker from the sticker sheet on the correct signpost on the poster.
4. Once your child has placed all eight signpost stickers, she has completed her journey and earned her Achievement Certificate.

BONUS FUN!

The colorful boardwalk poster is also a Hidden Pictures® puzzle! It is hiding 20 seashells for your child to find.

Each time your child finishes a chapter, add a sticker!

Place a sun sticker on each hidden seashell!

Use the emoji stickers to mark favorite activities in the book!

Contents

Each chapter covers a variety of subjects, so that kids will get practice in different curriculum areas throughout the summer to help prevent learning loss and bridge the gap between kindergarten and first grade.

- How to use this book 2–3
- Chapter 1 5
- Chapter 2 21
- Chapter 3 38
- Chapter 4 55
- Chapter 5 72
- Chapter 6 89
- Chapter 7 106
- Chapter 8 123
- Answers 140
- Achievement Certificate 144
- Reward Stickers
- Summer Big Fun Adventure Poster

Your Hidden Pictures® poster and stickers are at the back of this book!

CHAPTER 1

Hop to 100

Help Freddy hop from 1 to 100. Fill in the missing numbers. Then start at 10. Hop by tens and circle each number you land on.

1	2	3	4	5	6	7	8	9	10
11	12	13	14	15	16	17	18	19	20
21	22	23	24	25	26	27	28	29	30
31	32	33	34	35	36	37	38	39	40
41	42	43	35	45	46	47	48	49	50
51	52	53	54	55	56	57	58	59	60
61	62	63	64	65	66	67	68	69	70
71	72	73	74	75	76	77	78	79	80
81	82	83	84	85	86	87	88	89	90
91	92	93	94	95	96	97	98	99	100

Aa

Trace and write uppercase A and lowercase a.

Aa Aa A a

Trace this tongue twister. See if you can say it five times, fast!

Amy asked for apple juice.

Cross out the alligator that is different in each row.

The word **apple** begins with the short **a** sound.
The name **Amy** begins with the long **a** sound.

Say each word. Circle each word that begins with the short **a** sound. Draw a box around each word that begins with a long **a** sound. Then write each word.

ant

ant

acorn

acorn

axe

axe

arrow

arrow

apron

apron

alien

alien

0

1

Trace the number 0. Then write your own.

Trace the number 1. Then write your own.

How many birds do you see in each scene: 0, 1, 2, or 3?

1

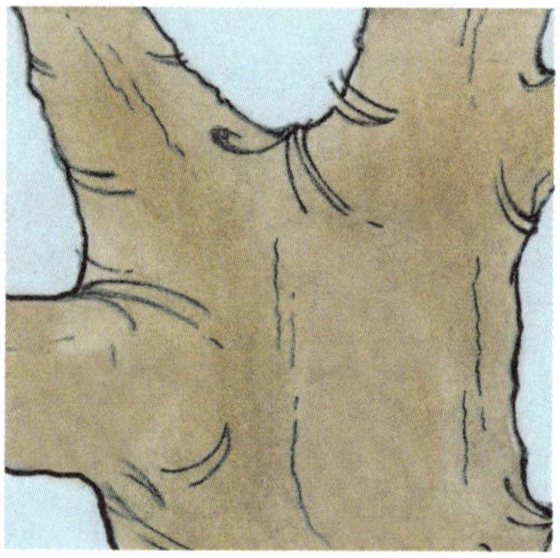

0

3

2

2

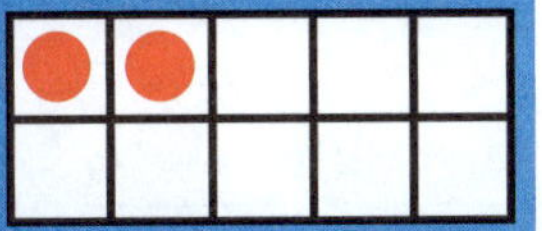

3

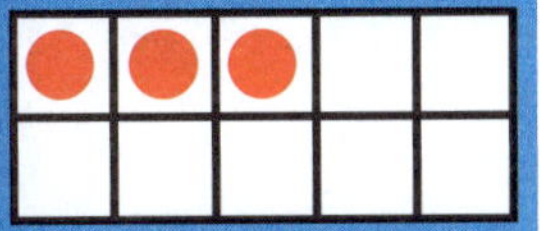

Trace the number 2. Then write your own.

Trace the number 3. Then write your own.

Find and count 1 worm, 2 blue cars, and 3 red flags.

Circle the numbers 1, 2, and 3 in the picture.

Bb

Trace and write uppercase **B** and lowercase **b**.

Bb

Trace this tongue twister. See if you can say it five times, fast!

Brian bought a blue bike.

Draw a line from each butterfly to its match.

It's Time to Rhyme!

Welcome to Silly Town's Flea Market. There's a star in a jar and a stork with a fork. What other rhyming things do you see?

How many balloons does the raccoon have?

4

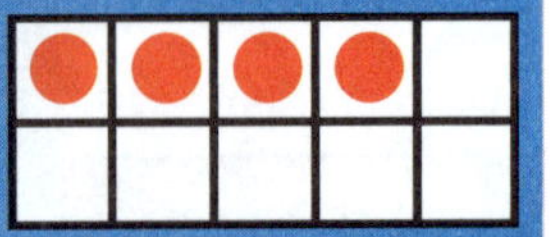

5

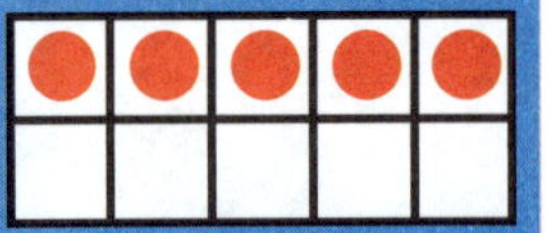

Trace the number 4. Then write your own.

4 4 4 4 4 4

Trace the number 5. Then write your own.

5 5 5 5 5 5

How many trucks are in each group?

6

5

4

7

6

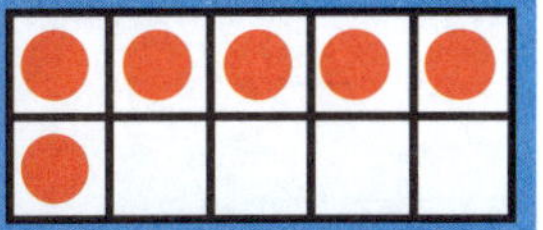

7

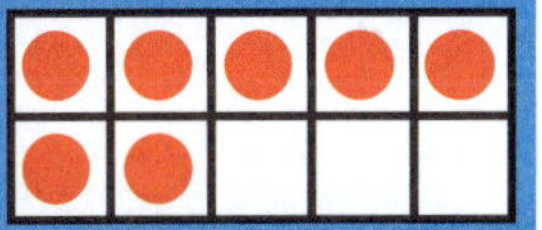

Trace the number **6**. Then write your own.

Trace the number **7**. Then write your own.

Find and count: **4** skateboards, **5** pairs of shorts, **6** in-line skates, and **7** helmets.

What are 3 words that rhyme with *skate*?

Cc

Trace and write uppercase C and lowercase c.

Cc

Trace this tongue twister. See if you can say it five times, fast!

Cassie carries crisp cookies.

How many C's can you find in this camel scene?

Shapes at the Beach

Cam and Carly see many shapes at the beach. Match the name of each shape they see by writing its number in the correct box.

1 circle 2 crescent 3 oval
4 rectangle 5 square 6 triangle

Dd

Trace and write uppercase **D** and lowercase **d**.

Dd

Trace this tongue twister. See if you can say it five times, fast!

Dragons danced after dinner.

Compare these 2 pictures. Can you find at least **10** differences?

What is a duck's favorite snack?

Cheese and quackers

Domino Match

Which dominoes have an equal number of dots? Draw a line to match each equal pair.

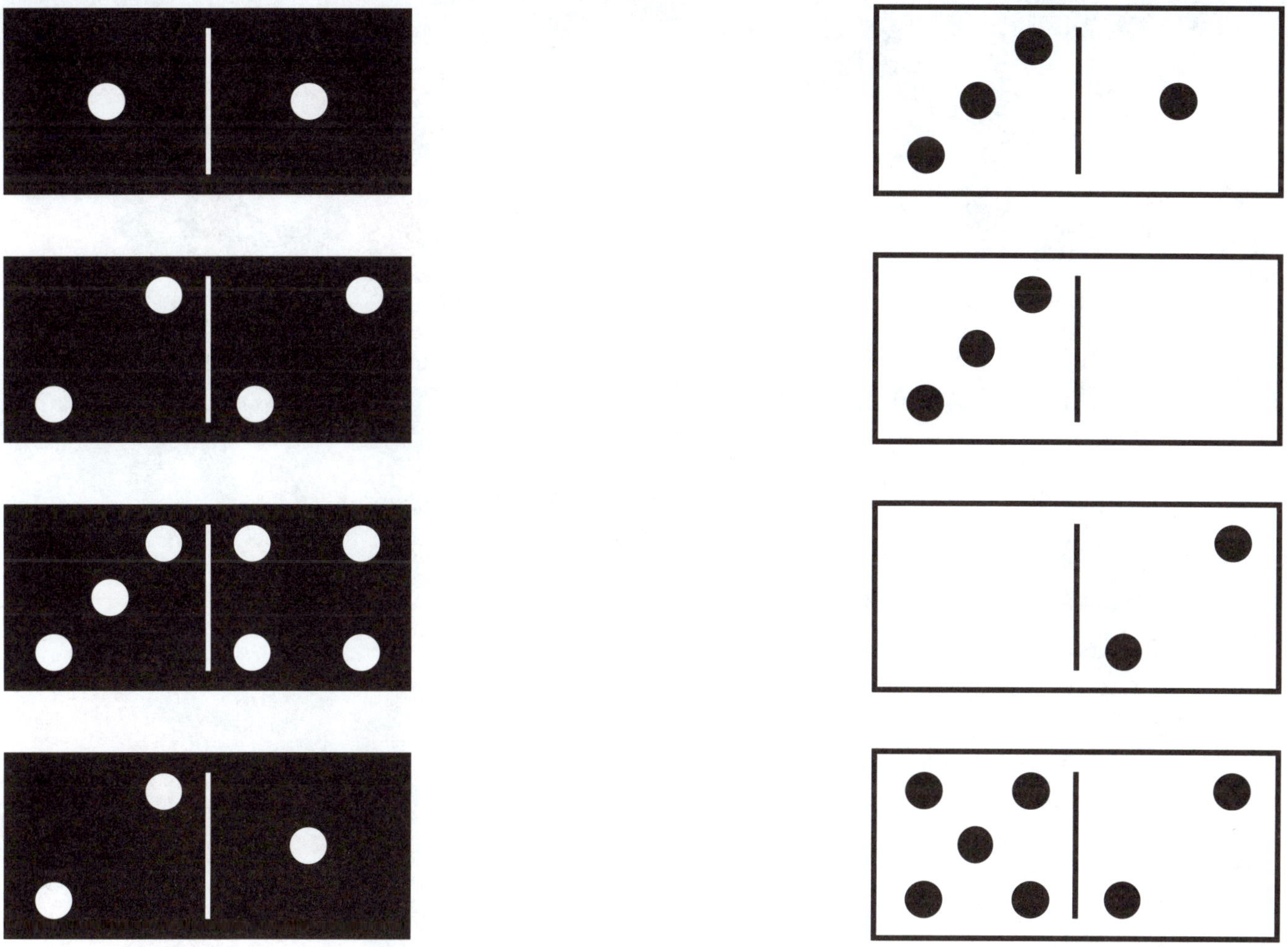

How many dots are on the black domino? Add dots to the white domino to make the two dominoes have an equal number of dots.

Color Campout

What colors do you see in this picture? Trace and say each color word on the next page. Then write the word. Can you find each color in this picture?

red

orange

yellow

green

blue

purple

black

white

pink

brown

Congratulations! You've completed **Chapter 1**. Place your Chapter 1 sticker on your poster. Try this activity, then start **Chapter 2**!

BONUS!
Summer Craft Activity

Nature's Palette

YOU WILL NEED:

- Pencil
- Old file folder
- Scissors
- Paint-sample strips
- Glue stick
- Construction paper

What time of the year do you think is the most colorful? Why?

1. With an adult's permission, use a pencil to draw the shape of a painter's palette like this one on the folder. Cut out the palette.

2. Cut out squares from the paint-sample strips. Glue them to the palette.

3. Go on a nature walk with the palette. Look for things in nature that match the colors on your palette.

4. After your walk, cut the remaining paint-sample strips into shapes. Glue them to construction paper to make a nature collage.

CHAPTER 2

Fruit Addition

Count the fruits in the first group and write the number. Count the fruits in the second group and write the number. How many fruits are there in all?

$\square + \square = \square$

$\square + \square = \square$

$\square + \square = \square$

$\square + \square = \square$

Ee

Trace and write uppercase **E** and lowercase **e**.

E e E e

Trace this tongue twister. See if you can say it five times, fast!

Eager Edgar exits leaping.

Help this eagle get to her eggs.

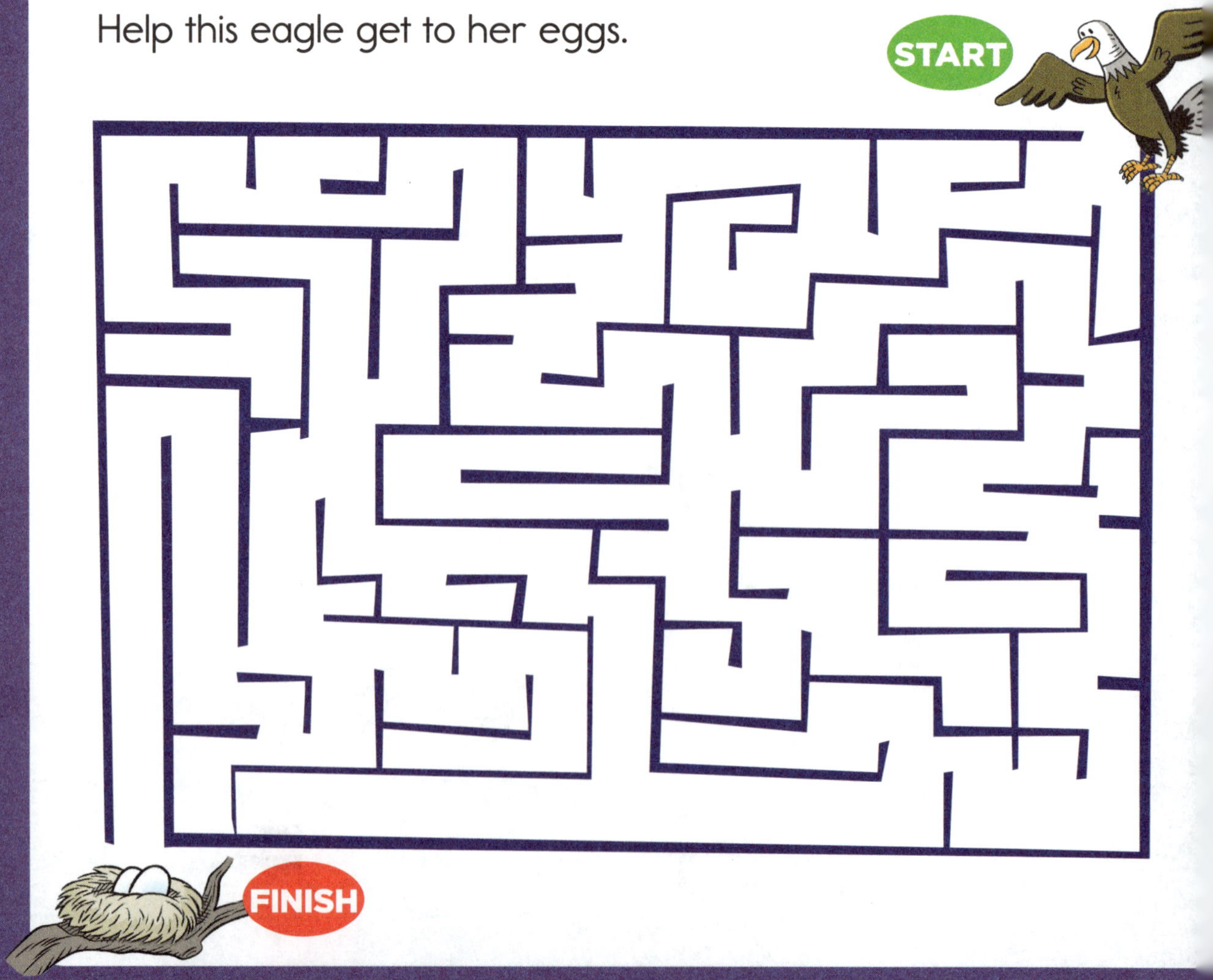

The word **egg** begins with the short **e** sound.
The word **eagle** begins with the long **e** sound.

Say each word. Circle each word that begins with the short **e** sound. Draw a box around each word that begins with a long **e** sound. Then write each word.

eat

elk

elephant

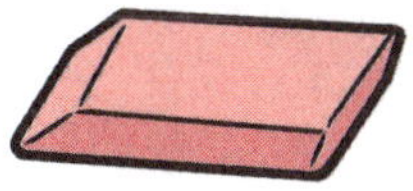

eraser

eel

elm

8

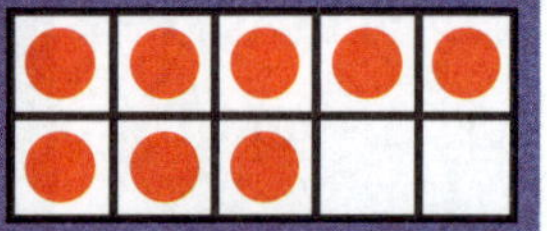

9

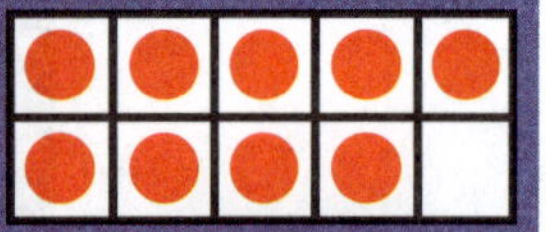

Trace the number 8. Then write your own.

8 8

Trace the number 9. Then write your own.

9 9

How many plates are in each stack? Cross off as you count.

10

Trace the number 10. Then write your own.

10 10

Countdown: 10 to 8. Can you find 10 bags of popcorn, 9 chairs, and 8 people wearing a hat or headband?

The word *popcorn* is hidden in the picture. Can you find it?

Ff

Trace and write uppercase **F** and lowercase **f**.

Ff Ff

Trace this tongue twister. See if you can say it five times, fast!

Fox finds five flowers.

Write **f** to complete the words.

__an

__ish

__lag

__rog

__ire__ly

More Fish?

Which row has 10 fish in all?

Circle the group in each row that has more fish.

Flying High

Fill in the missing numbers.

Which group has the most hot-air balloons?

How many hot-air balloons are in each group?

6

5

2

4

7

3

Silly Gardeners

Trace and say each word on the next page. Then write the word. Can you answer the questions about this picture?

Can you find the lollipop tree?

the

What is on the sunflower?

is

Do you see the boy and rabbit?

and

The girl is making a sandcastle.

a

The horse's rider wants an apple.

an

Gg

Trace and write uppercase G and lowercase g.

Gg Gg

Trace this tongue twister. See if you can say it five times, fast!

Gracie the goat grazes.

How many G's can you find in this picture?

Gumball Subtraction

Count the gumballs in all, and write the number. Count how many someone takes away, and write the number. How many are left?

4 − 2 = 2

2 − 1 = 1

5 − 2 = 3

3 − 1 = 2

4 − 3 = 1

Bears

Read the poem and then answer the questions.

Bears are bashful.
Bears are bright.
Polar bears are dressed in white.

Bears are playful.
Bears are round.
Grizzly bears are dressed
in brown.

Bears like honey.
Bears like trees.
Bears get chased by honeybees.

Bears like mountains.
Bears like streams.
Bears spend winters in
their dreams.

Which bears are white? Which bears are brown?

What chases bears?

What are two things that bears like?

Hh

Trace and write uppercase H and lowercase h.

Hh Hh

Trace this tongue twister. See if you can say it five times, fast!

Hedgehogs hop happily.

Each horse piñata has one that matches it exactly. Draw lines between the matching pairs.

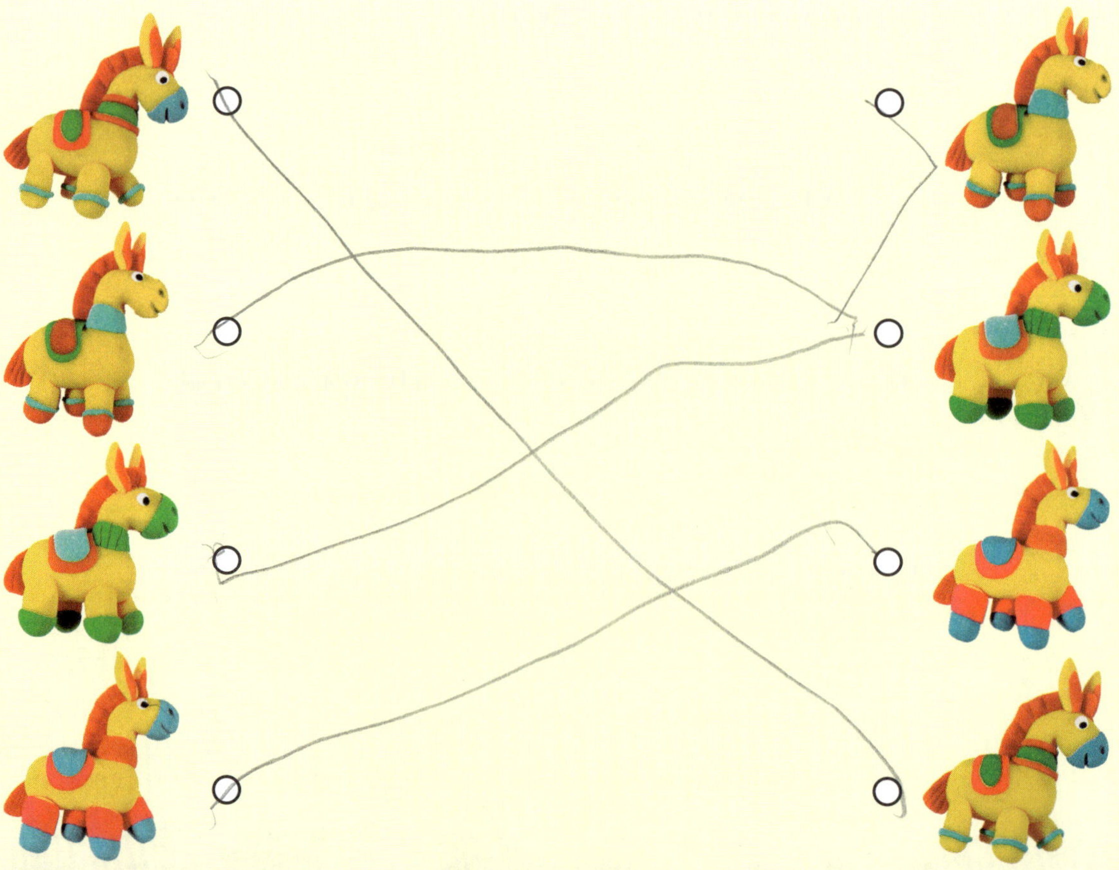

Congratulations! You've completed **Chapter 2**. Place your Chapter 2 sticker on your poster. Try this activity, then start **Chapter 3**!

BONUS! Summer Craft Activity

Treasure Map

YOU WILL NEED:

- Brown paper bag
- Markers
- Paintbrush
- Water

Hide a "treasure" for a friend or family member. Then make this map to lead him or her to it!

1. With an adult's permission, tear along the seam on the back of the bag. Tear off the bag's bottom. Crumple the paper.

2. Use markers to draw a map. Draw an X on one part of the map. Draw a path to the X.

3. Paint the map with water, spreading the colors. Let it dry.

4. On the back of the map, draw a picture of what someone will find when he or she reaches the X.

CHAPTER

3

Ii

Trace and write uppercase I and lowercase i.

I i I i

Trace this tongue twister. See if you can say it five times, fast!

Ivan inspects interesting insects.

How many I's can you find in this picture?

The word **insect** begins with the short **i** sound.
The name **Ivan** begins with the long **i** sound.

Say each word. Circle each word that begins with the short i sound. Draw a box around each word that begins with a long i sound. Then write each word.

iguana

igloo

island

iron

insect

ice cube

11

12

13

Trace each number and write your own. Then circle the group with that number.

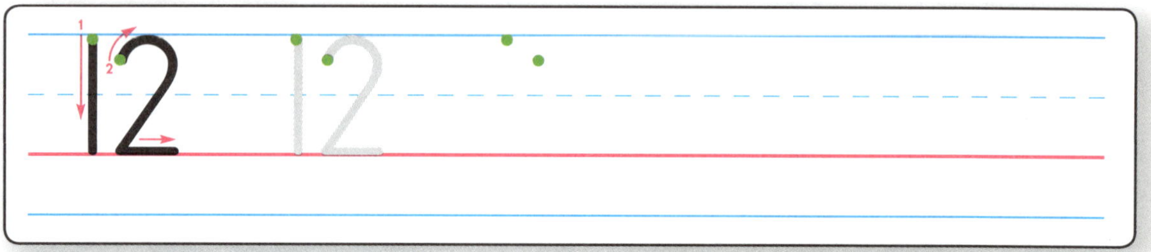

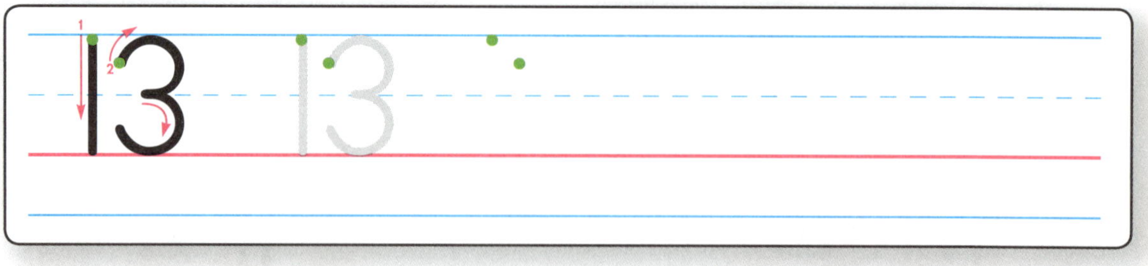

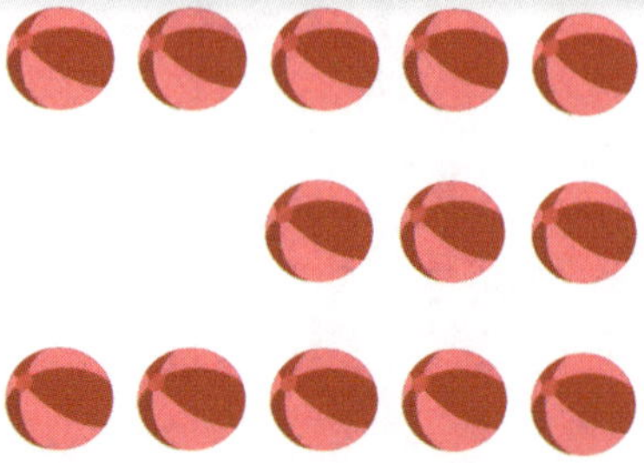

On the Ice

Knock, knock.
Who's there?
Icy.
Icy who?
Icy a big polar bear!

Count and circle 13 animals. How many animals are wearing hats? How many animals have ice skates?

J j

Trace and write uppercase J and lowercase j.

J j J j

Trace this tongue twister. See if you can say it five times, fast!

The jaguar just jumped.

Write j to complete the words.

__ellyfish

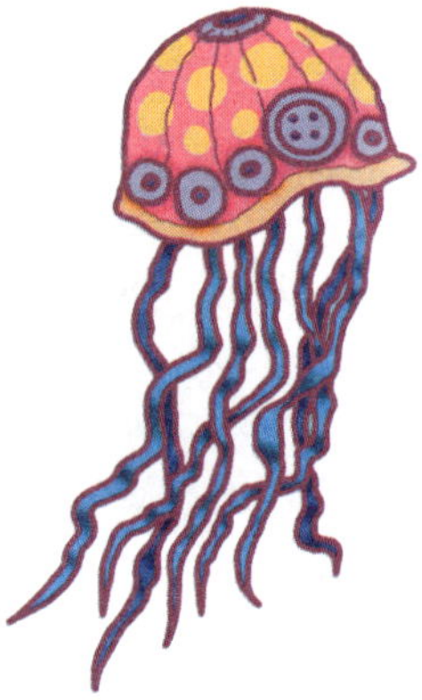

__ar

__ump rope

__eans

__uggle

Color by Sum

Solve each addition problem. Match the answer to a color in the color key. Then use markers or crayons to color the picture.

Fill-in Fun

Color each space that has the number 5 to see a sunny sight.

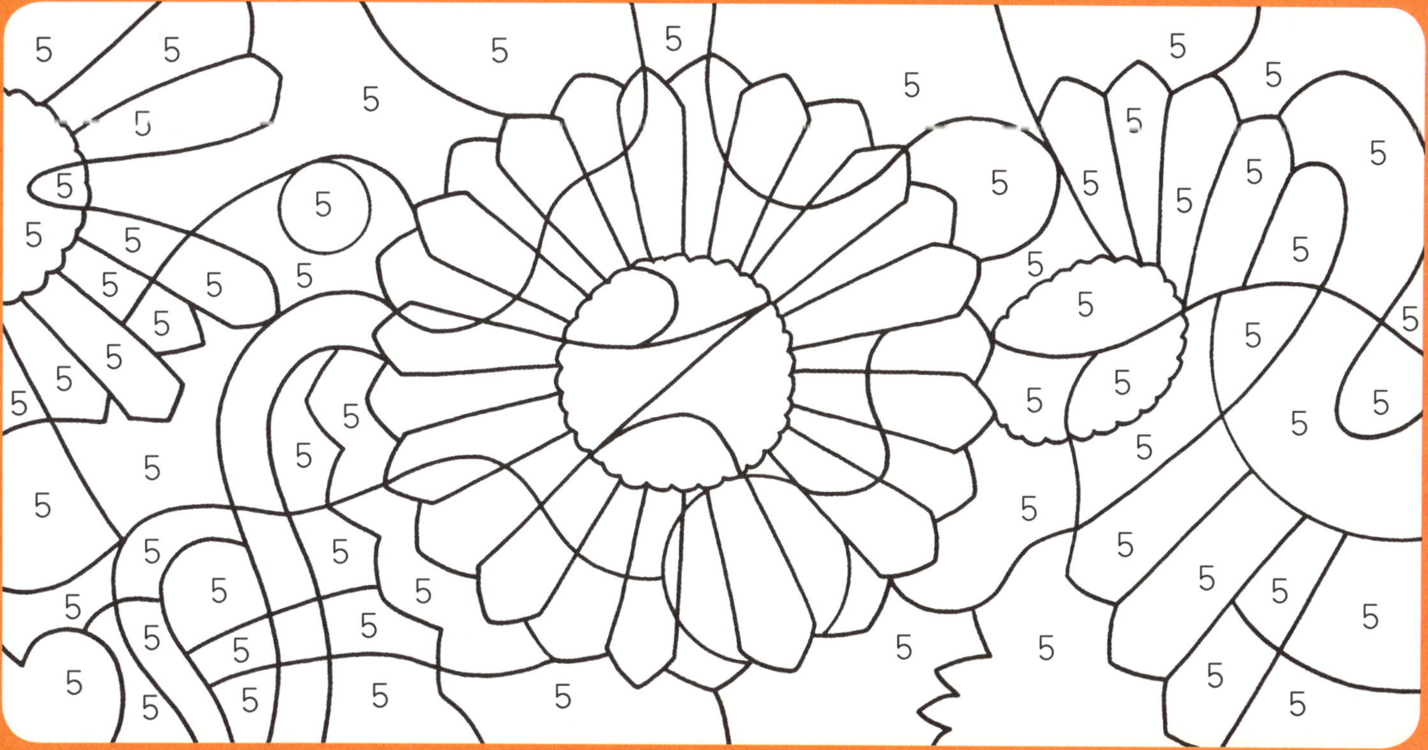

14

15

16

Trace each number and write your own. Then circle the group with that number.

14 14

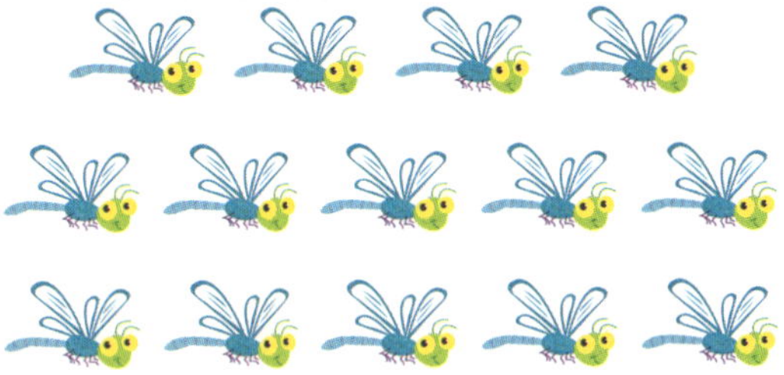

15 15

16 16

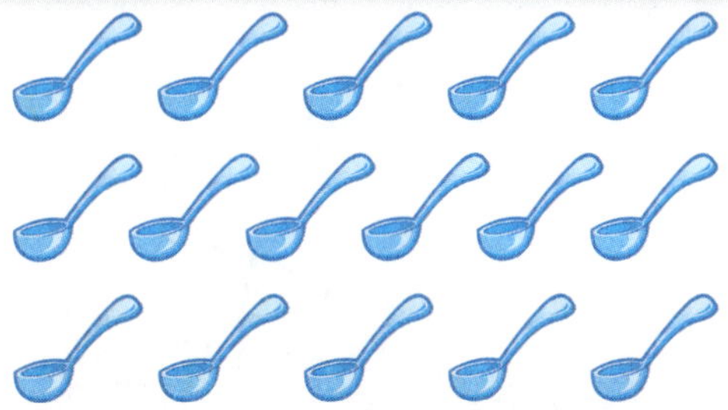

Jungle Gym

Find and count 14 animals. How many purple yoga blocks do you see? How many stars do you see? Cross off as you count.

Put an **X** on 10 silly things.

Kk

Trace and write uppercase K and lowercase k.

Kk Kk

Trace this tongue twister. See if you can say it five times, fast!

Kind Katie keeps a kitten.

Follow the string to find Kyle's kite.

What Doesn't Belong?

Cross out the object in each group that doesn't belong with the others.

goat

truck

pig

dog

broccoli

apple

key

cheese

Which Is Less?

Which row has 14 instruments in all?

Count the musical instruments in each group. Write the number in the space beside the group. Circle the number that is less.

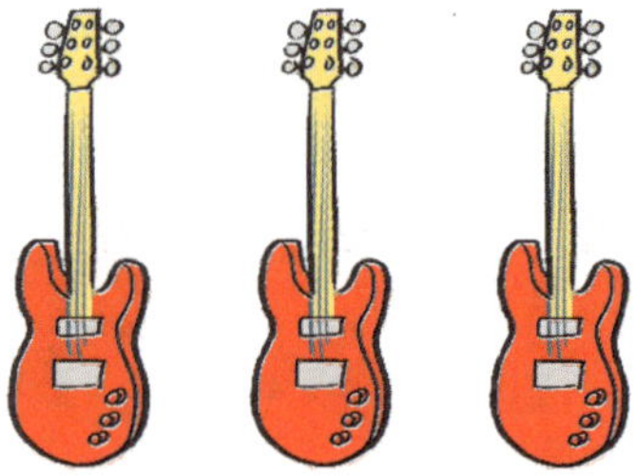

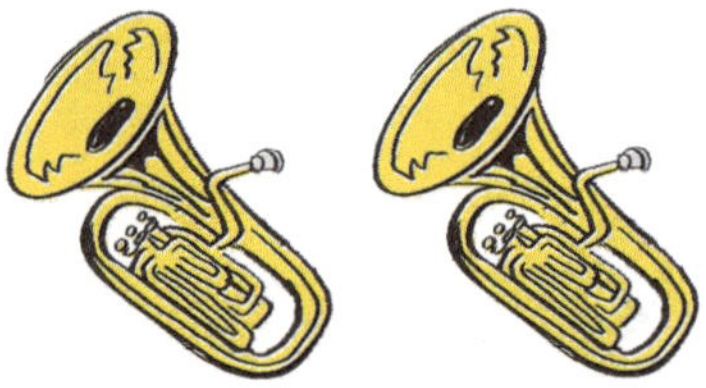

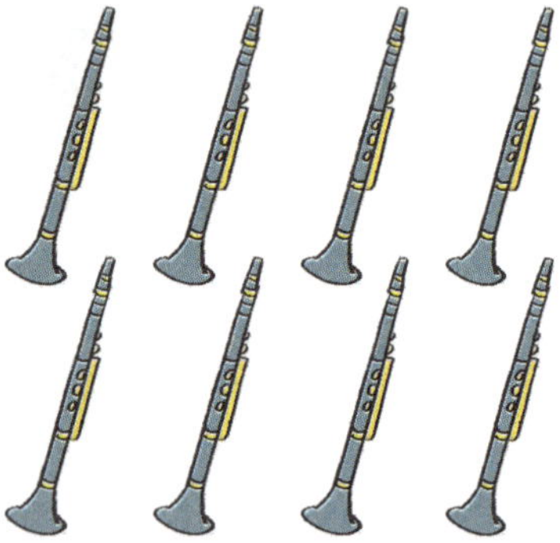

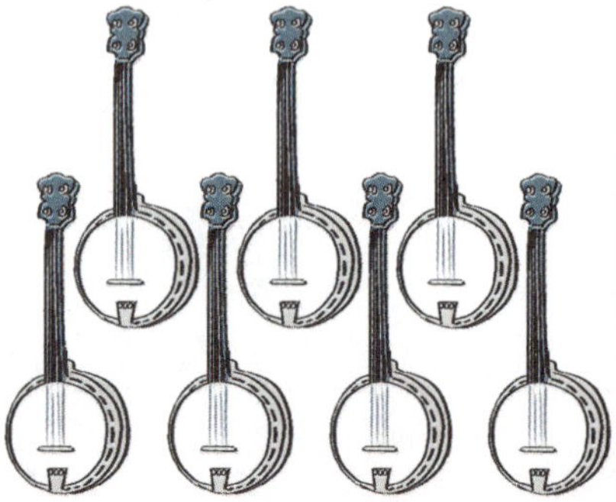

Color by Difference

Solve each subtraction problem. Match the answer to a color in the color key. Then use markers or crayons to color the picture.

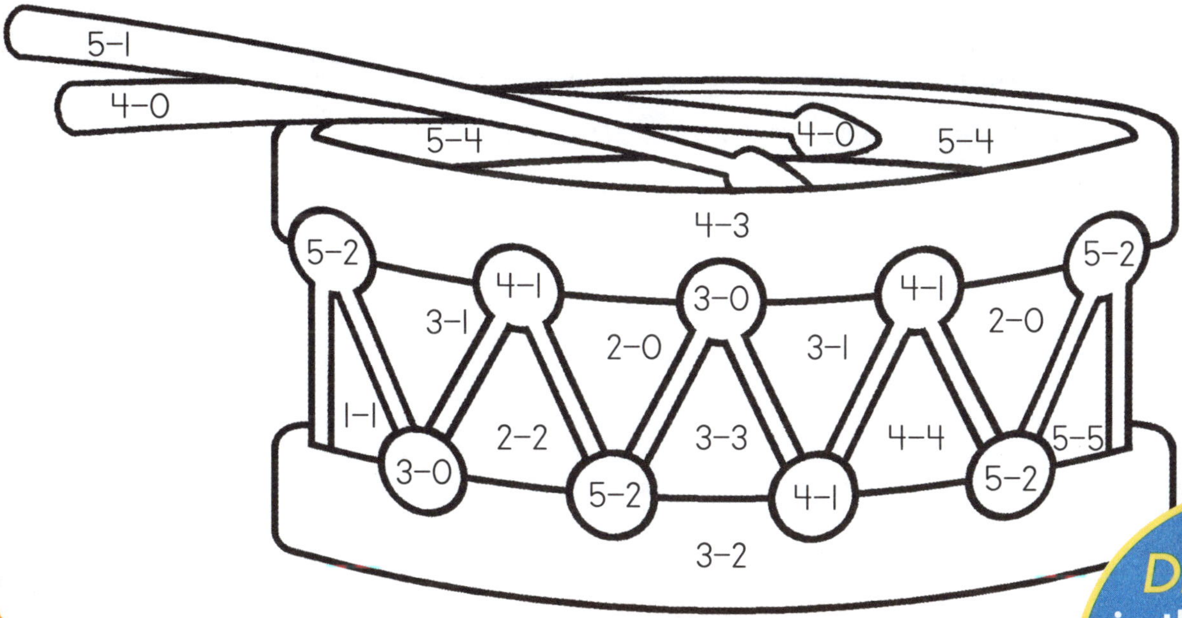

Difference **is the answer you get when you subtract.**

Fill-in Fun

Color each space that has the number 0 to see a night flyer.

Ll

Trace and write uppercase L and lowercase l.

L l L l

Trace this tongue twister. See if you can say it five times, fast!

Little Lizzie listens.

Copy these l words, and read them aloud.

leaf

lamb

lemon

lamp

Weigh In

Circle the vehicle that weighs the most.

Circle the animal that weighs the least.

Beach Day!

These friends are having a great time at the beach. Write a story about it on the next page. Then see if you can find the **8** objects in this Hidden Pictures® puzzle.

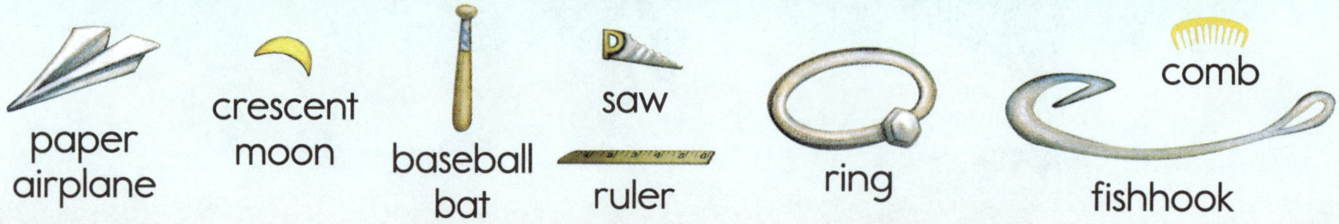

Include some of the words from the word box in your story.

cat	blue	dog
eat	spoon	water

The animals

Congratulations! You've completed **Chapter 3**. Place your Chapter 3 sticker on your poster. Try this activity, then start **Chapter 4**!

BONUS!
Summer Craft Activity

Paint Some Pots, Plant Some Seeds

YOU WILL NEED:

- Dot stickers
- Small terra-cotta pot
- Acrylic paint
- Paintbrushes
- Dirt
- Flower seeds
- Water

1. With an adult's permission, firmly press some dot stickers on the pot.

2. Cover the entire pot with acrylic paint. Allow it to dry overnight.

3. Remove the stickers to reveal your polka-dot pattern.

4. Fill the pot with dirt. Plant a few flower seeds. Add a little water and set the pot in a sunny spot.

Why do you think some plants grow faster than others?

CHAPTER 4

Mail Match

Help Milo the mail carrier deliver these packages. Solve each problem. Then draw a line from each package to the house that has the same sum.

$2 + 2 = \square$

$3 + 2 = \square$

$1 + \square = 3$

$0 + 3 = \square$

$0 + 1 = \square$

$2 + 0 = \square$

$1 + \square = 2$

$3 + 1 = \square$

$4 + 1 = \square$

$\square + 0 = 1$

Mm

Trace and write uppercase **M** and lowercase **m**.

Mm Mm

Trace this tongue twister. See if you can say it five times, fast!

A merry mouse

makes music.

Draw a line from each mitten to its match.

Monster Mania

The arrow of each symbol points to the smaller number.

Count the monsters. Write **<** (**less than**) or **>** (**greater than**) to show which group in each row is more or less. Read each equation from left to right, just like a sentence. For example, "4 is greater than 3."

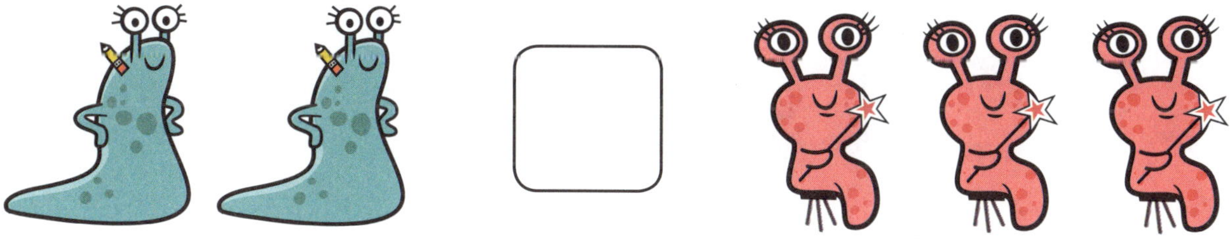

17

Trace each number and write your own. Then circle the group with that number.

17 17

18

18 18

19

19 19

20

20 20

Nn

Trace and write uppercase **N** and lowercase **n**.

Nn Nn

Trace this tongue twister. See if you can say it five times, fast!

Nancy counts nine nuts.

Write **n** to complete the words.

__est

__ap

__ickel

__et

__otebook

Almost the Same

Read each word. Write two words from the box that have almost the same meaning.

Think about the shades of meaning for the words in each group. How are they different? Act it out!

jump	leap	peek
shout	stare	whisper

look

hop

say

On the Farm

Help Bonnie find her way to her friends. Follow the path from **0** to **20** and fill in the missing numbers along the way. Now find and count **20** sunflowers in the picture.

Are there more pigs or sheep? Cross off as you count.

Oo

Trace and write uppercase O and lowercase o.

O o O o

Trace this tongue twister. See if you can say it five times, fast!

Olivia and Ollie love the ocean.

Help this octopus get to the ocean.

The word **odd** begins with the short **o** sound.
The word **over** begins with the long **o** sound.

Say each word. Circle each word that begins with the short **o** sound. Draw a box around each word that begins with a long **o** sound. Then write each word.

oval

ostrich

otter

oboe

old

oven

Pp

Trace and write uppercase **P** and lowercase **p**.

Pp Pp

Trace this tongue twister. See if you can say it five times, fast!

Patty Peacock picks paints.

Cross out the penguin that is different in each row.

Penny Addition

What did one penny say to the other penny? *Together we make cents!*

Count the pennies in the first group and write the number. Count the pennies in the second group and write the number. How many pennies are there in all?

$\square + \square = \square$

$\square + \square = \square$

$\square + \square = \square$

$\square + \square = \square$

Finding a Home

Read the story and then answer the questions.

Like snails and turtles, hermit crabs need shells to stay safe. But they do not have shells of their own. They must find empty shells that will be just right.

The shell can't be too big. The shell can't be too heavy to carry as the crab scuttles around the shoreline. The shell can't be too small. The crab needs to fit all the way inside the shell when danger comes.

This hermit crab found an old sea-snail shell. It fits just right! The crab can easily carry its new home wherever it goes.

Why does a hermit crab need a shell?

How does a hermit crab get a new shell?

Why is the size of a shell important to a hermit crab?

Shape Art

Use the shapes below to draw a picture. You can change the size and color of your shapes. Then use shapes to decorate the frame.

Congratulations! You've completed **Chapter 4**. Place your Chapter 4 sticker on your poster. Try this activity, then start **Chapter 5**!

BONUS!
Summer Fun Recipe

Flags for Breakfast

What is your favorite meal of the day? Why?

YOU WILL NEED:

- Whole-wheat bread
- Cream cheese
- Strawberry jam
- Blueberries
- Milk

1. With an adult's help, toast slices of whole-wheat bread. Spread cream cheese on the toast.
2. Add strawberry-jam stripes and blueberry stars.
3. Serve it with milk for a patriotic breakfast.

Bird Count

How many blue birds are there? How many red birds? How many yellow birds?

Count the number of birds in each group. Write the number. Then color the boxes to show how many birds there are of each color. Which group has the most birds? Which group has the fewest birds?

How many more purple birds are there than green birds?

Qq

Trace and write uppercase Q and lowercase q.

Qq Qq

Trace this tongue twister. See if you can say it five times, fast!

Quinn is the quickest quail.

How many Q's can you find in this picture?

Number Quilt

Complete this number quilt. Add the symbol **>** (**greater than**), **<** (**less than**) or **=** (**equal to**) to tell about each set of numbers. Remember that the arrow points to the smaller number.

Playground Cats

Trace and say each red word on the next page. Then write the word.
Can you answer the questions about this picture?

What is near the tree?

near

What is the yellow cat in?

in

A gray cat swings under the bars.

under

The napping cat is on the seesaw.

on

A black kitten hangs down.

down

Rr

Trace and write uppercase **R** and lowercase **r**.

Rr Rr

Trace this tongue twister. See if you can say it five times, fast!

Rhinos rarely run.

Draw a line from each rooster to one that matches it exactly.

Fact Family Rocket

Use markers or crayons to decorate the rocket.

The numbers **2**, **3**, and **5** form a fact family. Solve these problems that make up the family.

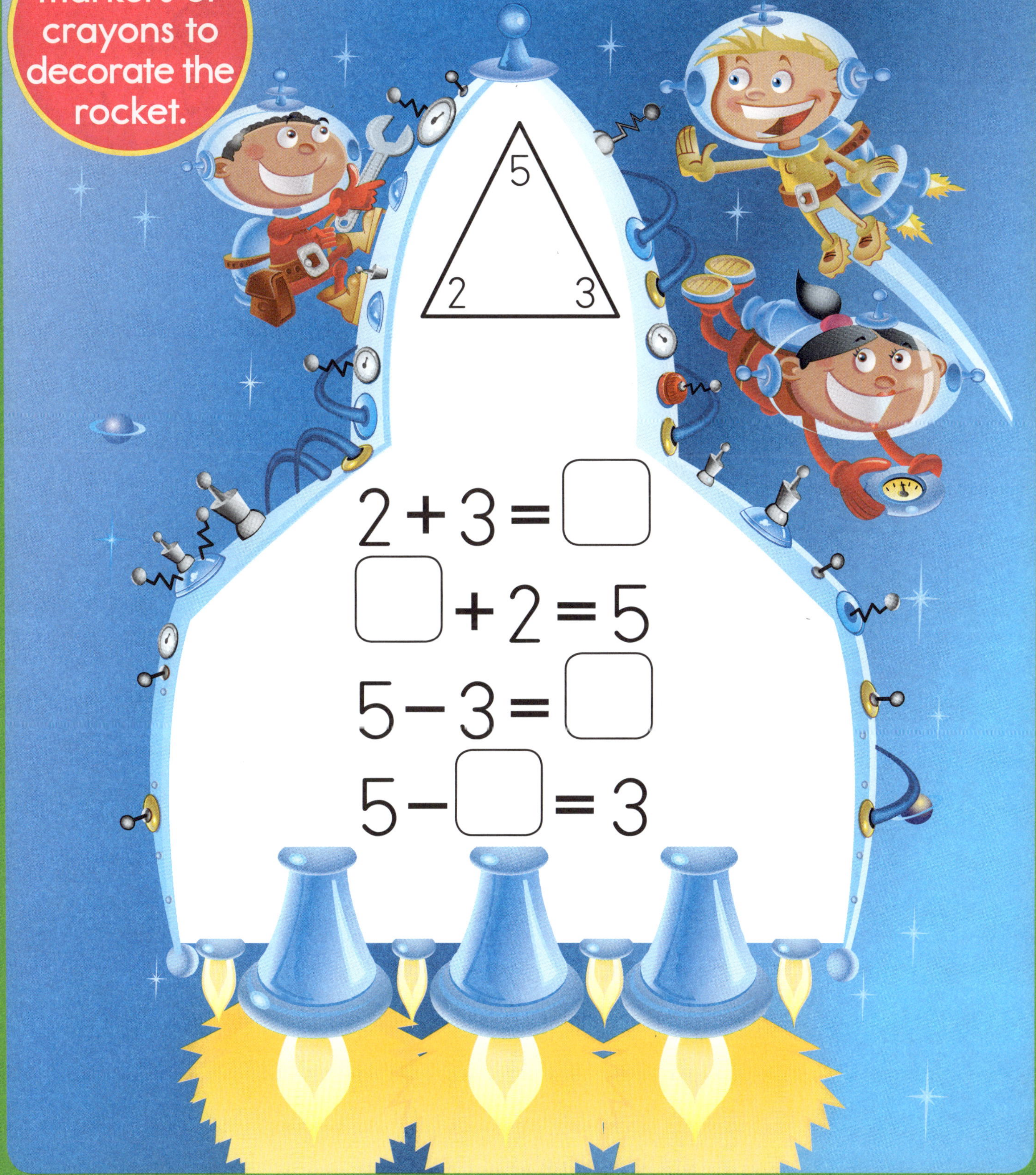

$2 + 3 = \square$

$\square + 2 = 5$

$5 - 3 = \square$

$5 - \square = 3$

Long or Short?

Rachel and her brother Ricky are playing mini-golf. Compare each set of objects they see on the golf course.

Circle the longest golf club.

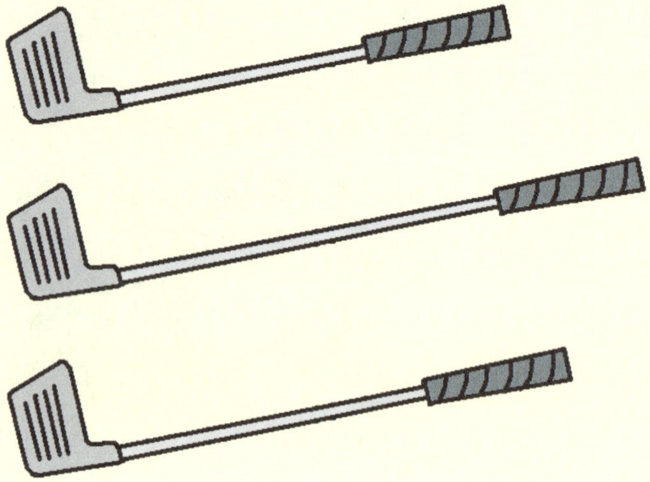

Circle the shortest path between the golf ball and the hole.

Tall or Short?

Circle the tallest lighthouse.

Circle the shortest windmill.

Ss

Trace and write uppercase **S** and lowercase **s**.

Ss Ss

Trace this tongue twister. See if you can say it five times, fast!

Sally Swan
swam solo.

Help Sylvie Snail get to Samuel Snail.

Sheep Subtraction

Count the sheep in each group and write the number.
Count how many walk away and write the number.
How many sheep are left?

Which group has the most sheep left after some walk away? Circle the group.

8 − 2 = 6

___ − ___ = ___

___ − ___ = ___

___ − ___ = ___

___ − ___ = ___

Which Word?

Complete each sentence using a word from the box.

catch	catches	hop
hops	swim	swims

Anna __________ in the big pool.

The girls __________ the water balloons.

Eli __________ over the short fence.

The bunnies __________ on the grass.

Mom and I __________ in the ocean.

The puppy __________ the ball.

Which Word?

Base words are stand-alone words that have meaning all by themselves.

Circle the word that answers the question.
Then underline the base word in each red word.

Which word means to become less strong?

weakest   weaken

Which word means someone who finishes last in a group?

slower   slowest

Which word means to take a lot of care?

careful   careless

Which word means to make something hot again?

preheat   reheat

Which word means the door is not bolted?

unlocked   relocked

Who Uses What?

Match each object to the correct worker.

 book ○		○ firefighter 	
 letter ○		○ crossing guard 	
 fire truck ○		○ doctor 	
 stop sign ○		○ mail carrier 	
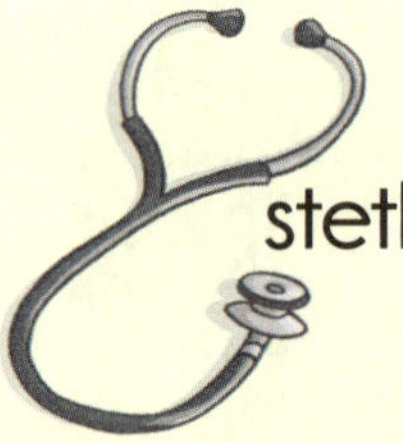 stethoscope ○		○ librarian 	

Choose a worker from page 86. What facts do you know about that worker's job? Write about what you know.

Congratulations! You've completed **Chapter 5**. Place your Chapter 5 sticker on your poster. Try this activity, then start **Chapter 6**!

BONUS! Summer Craft Activity

Paint with Sand

YOU WILL NEED:

- Sand
- Small jars with lids
- Food coloring
- Glue
- Cardboard

Find a place to work outside or cover a table with newspaper.

1. With an adult's permission, put sand into jars. Add a few drops of food coloring. Put the lids on, and shake the jars.

2. Put glue on the cardboard. Sprinkle sand on the glue.

3. Wait 15 minutes. Gently shake the cardboard over a trash container. You've made art from sand!

What color will you get by mixing red and blue food coloring? How about red and yellow?

CHAPTER 6

What's Out?

Cross out the object in each group that doesn't belong with the others.

Tiny Creatures

Which animals on this page start with the letter **s**?

Solve each addition problem. How many more little animals do you need? Draw a circle for each animal you need in the space below the problem.

$10 + \square = 11$

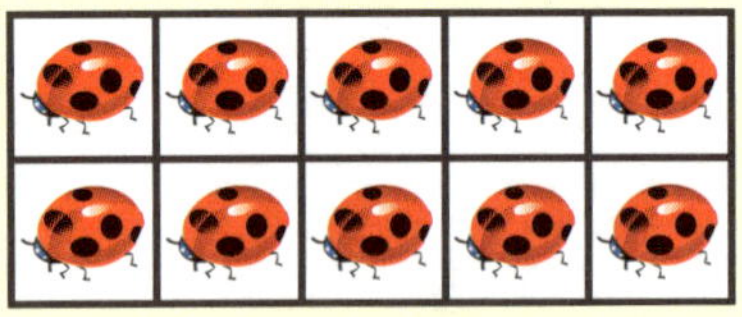

$10 + \square = 12$

$10 + \square = 13$

What is your favorite small animal?

13 = 10 + 3

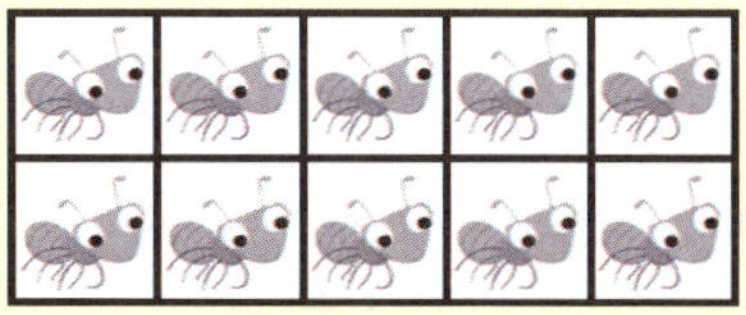

12 = 10 + 2

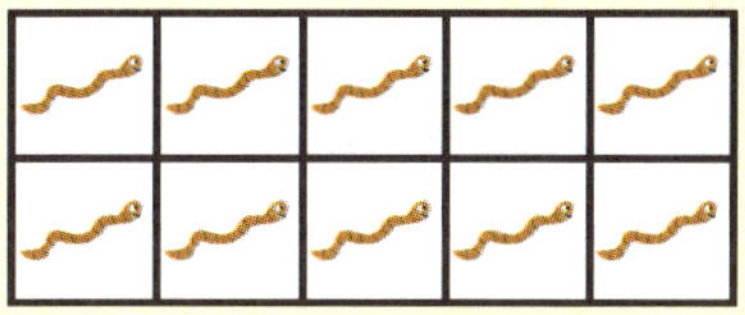

11 = 10 + 1

Tt

Trace and write uppercase **T** and lowercase **t**.

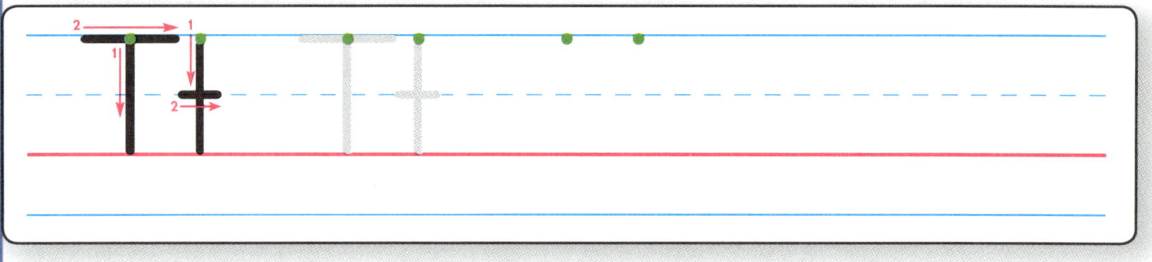

Trace this tongue twister. See if you can say it five times, fast!

Two toucans
take turns.

Circle the two toy train engines that match exactly.

Moose Games

A **3-D shape** is solid. This cube is a 3-D shape.

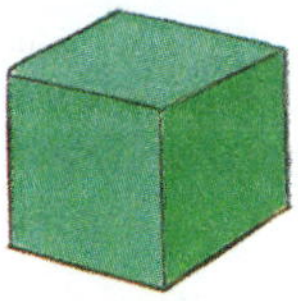

A **2-D shape** is flat. This square is a 2-D shape.

Help Mort find where Murray is hiding.
Follow only the 2-D shapes from start to finish.
You can only move left, right, up, or down.

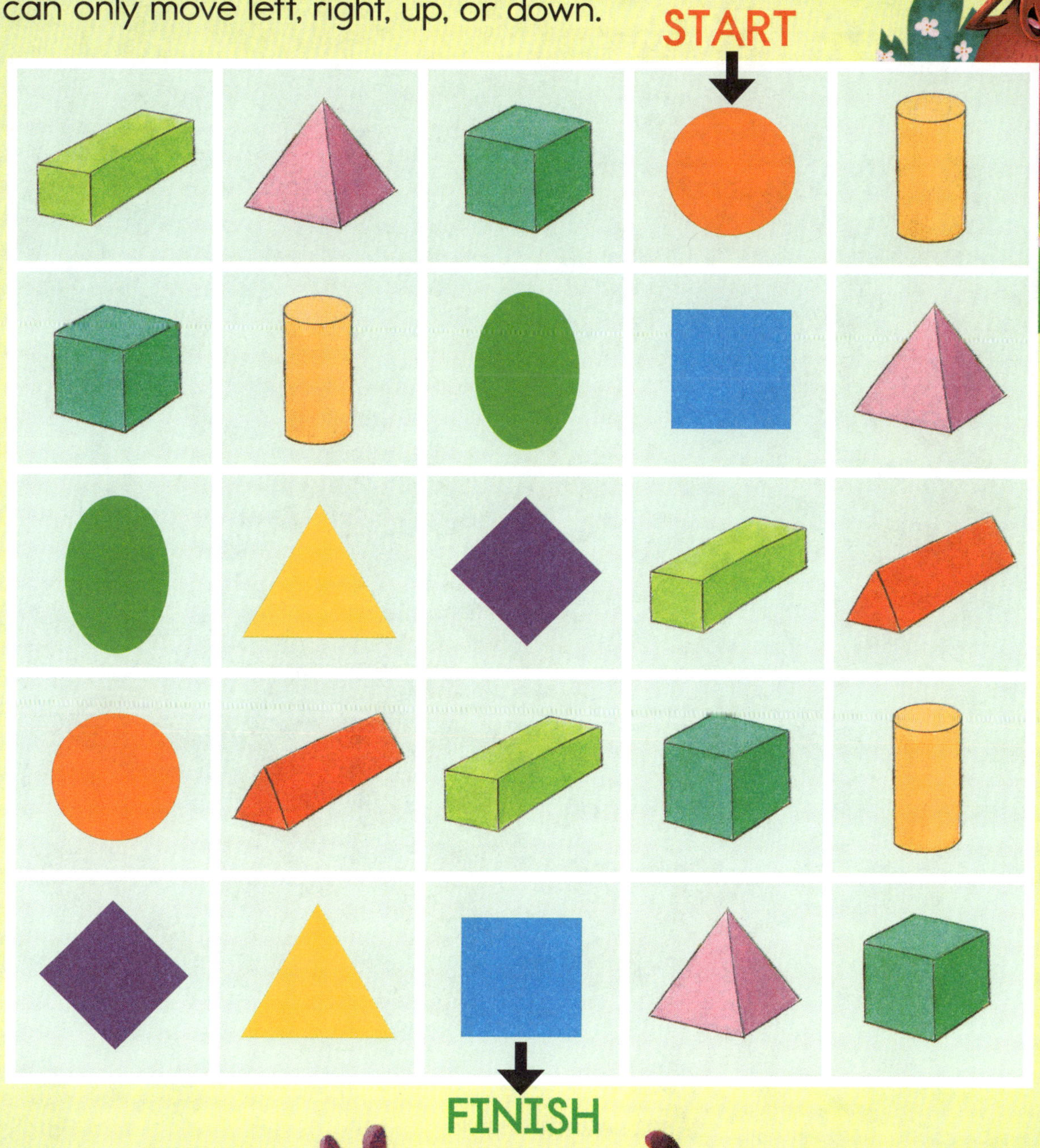

Here We Go!

Trace and say each red word on the next page. Then write the words and read the sentences about this picture. Now see if you can find the **6** objects in this Hidden Pictures® puzzle.

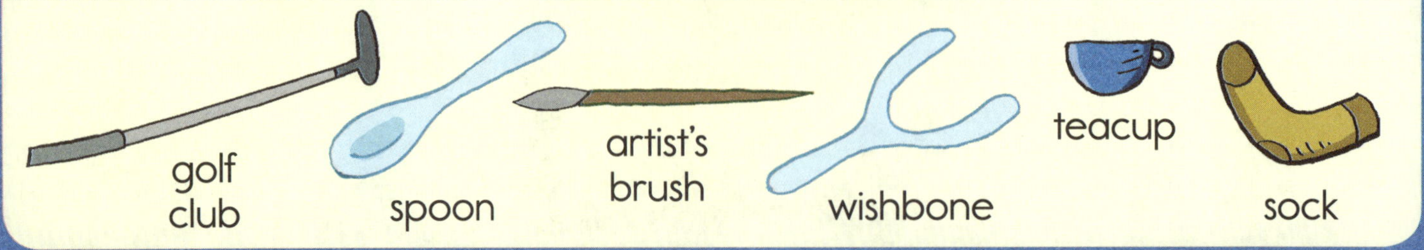

The friends are inside the raft.

inside

The raft rushes through the water.

through

Fox sits behind Deer.

behind

Raccoon sits in the front of the raft.

front

What does the animal beside the fox do?

beside

Uu

Trace and write uppercase **U** and lowercase **u**.

Uu Uu

Trace this tongue twister. See if you can say it five times, fast!

Uncle Ulric
uses a utensil.

Draw a line from each umbrella to its match.

The word **uncle** begins with the short **u** sound.
The word **utensil** begins with the long **u** sound.

Say each word. Circle each word that begins with the short u sound. Draw a box around each word that begins with a long u sound. Then write each word.

unicorn

uniform

umpire

unicycle

umbrella

upset

Under the Ocean

Bruce went snorkeling in the ocean. Solve the word problems below to find out how many animals he saw.

Bruce saw **3** seahorses. Then **1** more seahorse swam by. How many seahorses did Bruce see all together?

3 + 1 = 4

Bruce saw **2** large stingrays and **1** small stingray. How many stingrays did he see all together?

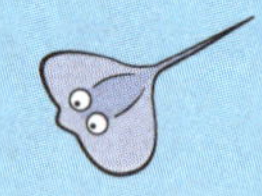

□ + □ = □

Bruce saw **1** orange fish and **4** blue fish. How many fish did he see all together?

□ + □ = □

Umbrellas for Sale

Jude has an umbrella stand. Solve the word problems below about the umbrellas he sold today.

Jude had **5** red umbrellas. He sold **2** red umbrellas. How many red umbrellas are left?

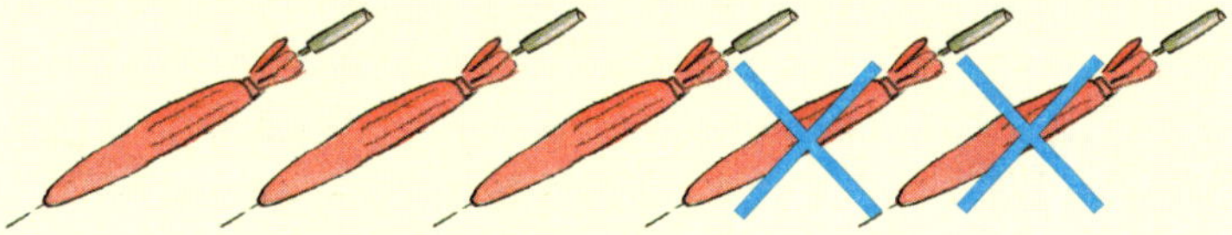

5 − 2 = 3

Jude had **3** green umbrellas. He sold **3** green umbrellas. How many green umbrellas are left?

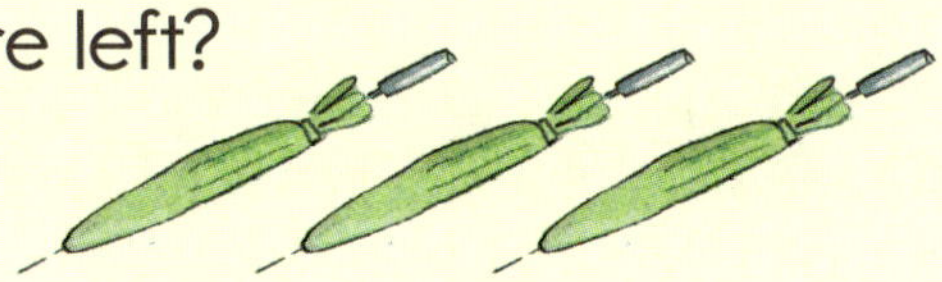

☐ − ☐ = ☐

Jude had **4** purple umbrellas. He sold **2** purple umbrellas. How many purple umbrellas are left?

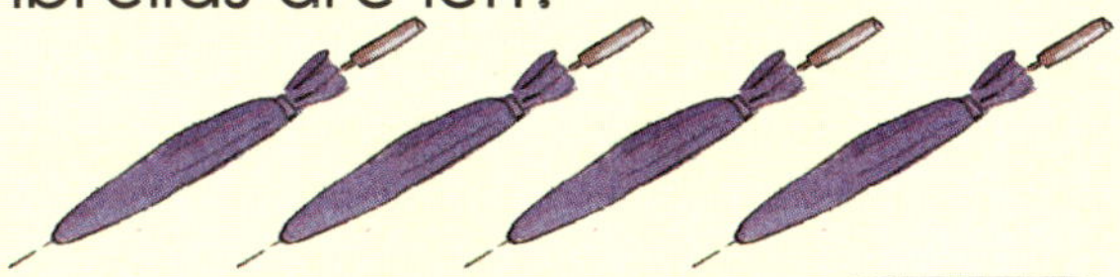

☐ − ☐ = ☐

BONUS PROBLEM: Fiona Flamingo had **3** dollars. She spent **2** dollars on an umbrella. How many dollars does she have left?

Vv

Trace and write uppercase V and lowercase v.

Vv Vv

Trace this tongue twister. See if you can say it five times, fast!

Vic's vest is very violet.

Help Val get her valentines to the mailbox.

Vacation Time

What is your favorite place to visit? Why?

Help Victor's family reach their vacation spot. Follow the arrows. Draw the symbol > (greater than), < (less than), or = (equal to) to complete each problem along the way.

Bang! Clang!

Read the story and then answer the questions.

Bang! Clang! Big dump truck! *Beep, beep, beep.* It's backing up.

The truck is orange. Its load is black. "Careful, kids. Stay safe. Step back."

The truck bed tilts. Tar is spilled. Shovels scrape. Holes are filled.

The work is done—nice and neat. The dump truck rumbles down the street.

Big Dump Truck!

What sounds does the truck make?

Who is watching the dump truck?

Where does this story take place? How do you know?

Shape to Shape

Which shapes have four sides?

Name each shape below. Draw a line from each shape to its match.

Congratulations! You've completed **Chapter 6**. Place your Chapter 6 sticker on your poster. Try this activity, then start **Chapter 7**!

BONUS! Summer Craft Activity

Pool-Noodle Village

Why do you think pool noodles have a hole in the center?

YOU WILL NEED:

- Scissors
- Pool noodle
- Colored duct tape
- Markers or crayons
- Cone-shaped paper cups
- Construction paper
- Clear tape

1. Ask an adult to cut a pool noodle into 4- and 5-inch sections. Cut pieces of colored duct tape to make windows and doors. Add details with markers, if desired.

2. To make a roof, decorate a cone-shaped cup with markers or crayons. Or cut a circle out of construction paper, cut out a section as shown here, and form a cone. Use tape to hold it together.

3. Put a roof on top of the pool-noodle house. Repeat these steps to build a pool-noodle village.

CHAPTER 7

Space Travel

Anna the astronaut is off to space! Count the different objects she sees, crossing off as you go. Draw tally marks in the chart to show how many.

Draw something else Anna might see in space.

Tally marks show how many.				
|	||	|||	||||	𝍸
1	2	3	4	5
𝍸 |	𝍸 ||	𝍸 |||	𝍸 ||||	𝍸 𝍸
6	7	8	9	10

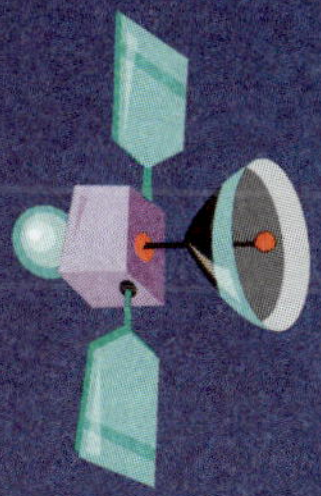

Object	Tally

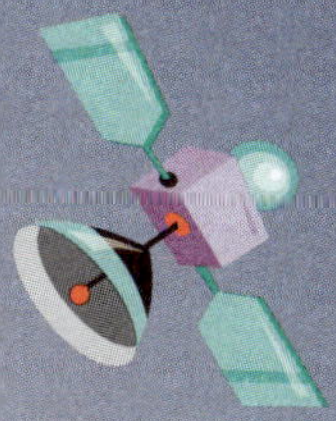

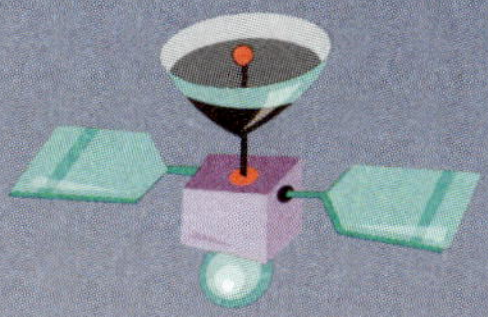

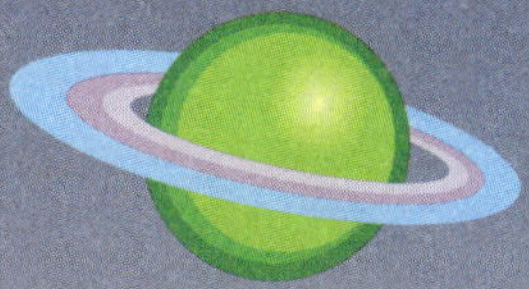

In the Woods

Circle all the differences you see between these pictures. Then read the sentences about the pictures. Trace and say each red word. Then write the word.

Which animals are in both pictures?

What is happening in the woods?

What

Some insects play music.

play

Many animals dance.

dance

A rabbit dances with a raccoon.

with

Every animal is having fun!

Every

Fact Family Flip Flops

Solve the addition and subtraction problems to complete each fact family.

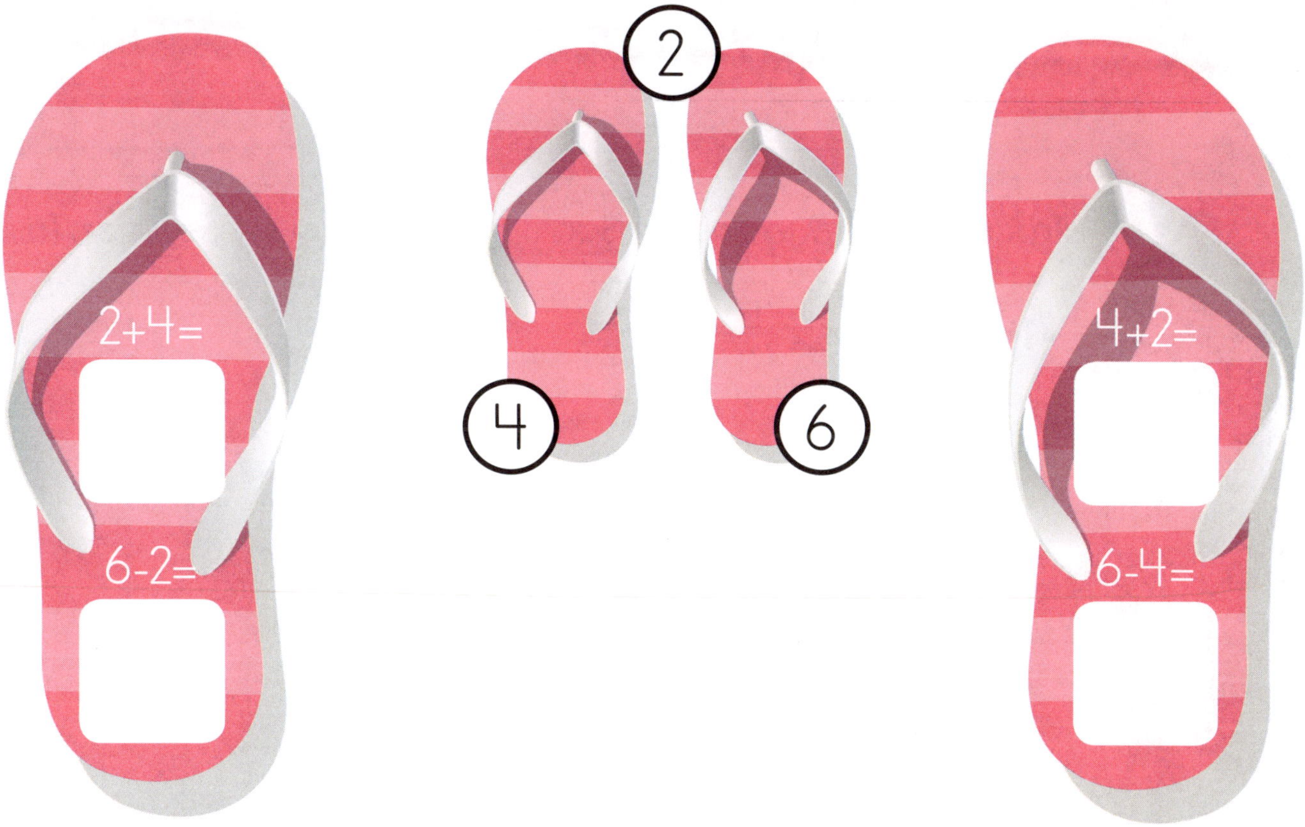

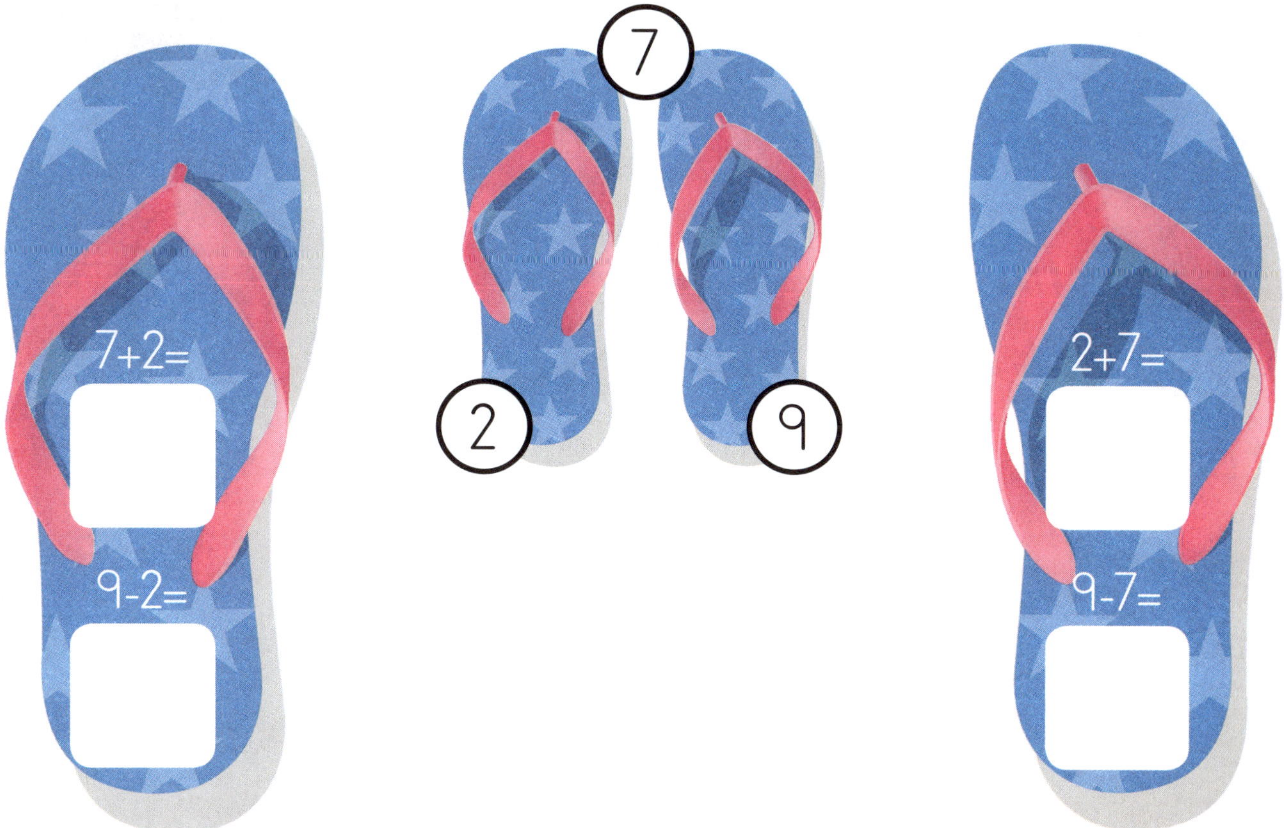

Ww

Trace and write uppercase W and lowercase w.

Ww Ww

Trace this tongue twister. See if you can say it five times, fast!

Wanda the
Whale wandered.

Write w to complete the words.

__agon

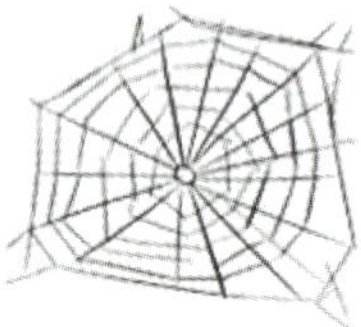

__eb

__heel

__alrus

__alking

The Big Roundup

Cowboy Bob has work to do! Solve the word problems below to help him figure out how many animals he has in each pen. We did one to get you started.

There were **3** cows in the cow pen. Then **3** more cows walked in. How many cows are in the pen now?

3 + 3 = 6

There were **6** sheep in the sheep pen. Then **4** more sheep walked in. How many sheep are in the pen now?

☐ + ☐ = ☐

There were **4** pigs in the pig pen. Then **5** more pigs walked in. How many pigs are in the pen now?

☐ + ☐ = ☐

BONUS QUESTION: Which pen now has the most animals in it?

What's It Like?

You can measure how tall or wide something is.

What are these dinosaurs like? Match each dinosaur with **2** words that tell about it. Then circle the words that are things you could measure. We did the first one for you.

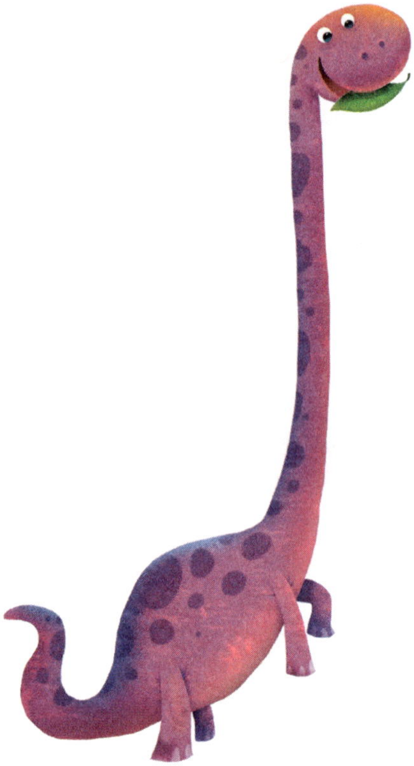

- purple
- short
- orange
- tall
- wide
- blue

Draw and color 2 more dinosaurs. What words tell about each one? What are things you could measure about the dinosaurs?

What's as big as a dinosaur but weighs nothing?
Its shadow!

Xx

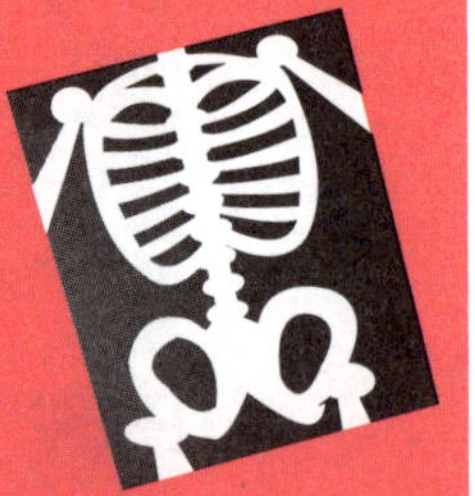

Trace and write uppercase X and lowercase x.

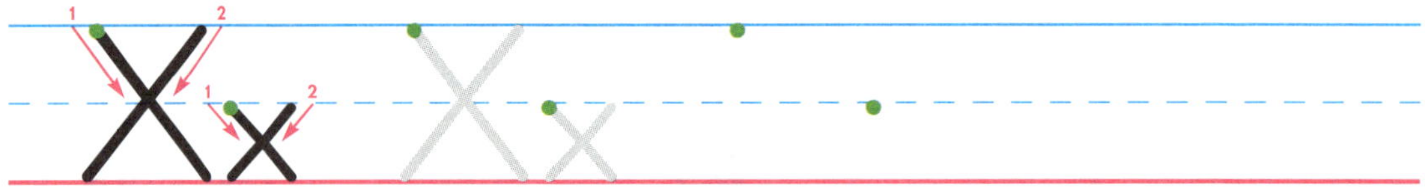

Trace this tongue twister. See if you can say it five times, fast!

Xavier's X-ray is in the box.

Help Max get to the taxi.

Grid Maze

To make your way from START to FINISH, solve the first subtraction problem (9-3). Draw a line to the answer (6). Then move to the next pair of numbers and do the same. Answers may be to the left, right, up, or down.

Just Add Food!

Solve each addition problem. How many more of each food item do you need? Draw a circle for each food you need in the space below the problem. Then write the number to complete the equation.

$$10 + \square = 14$$

$$10 + \square = 15$$

$$10 + \square = 16$$

16 = 10 + ☐

15 = 10 + ☐

14 = 10 + ☐

What Do You Think?

Think about a book you know. Draw something you liked from the book.

Write about your drawing. Tell why you liked the part of the book that you drew.

Congratulations! You've completed **Chapter 7**. Place your Chapter 7 sticker on your poster. Try this activity, then start **Chapter 8**!

BONUS! Summer Craft Activity

Let's Make Binoculars!

What would you like to look at through binoculars?

YOU WILL NEED:

- 2 Bathroom-tissue tubes
- Stickers
- Markers
- Tape
- Hole punch
- Yarn

Binoculars are special glasses that make faraway things seem to be closer. Here's how to make some pretend binoculars.

1. With an adult's permission, decorate the tubes.

2. Tape the tubes together.

3. Punch a hole in each tube.

4. Thread a piece of yarn through each hole and tie a knot.

CHAPTER 8

Strong Words

Think about the meanings of the words in each box. Then write the words in order to show their meanings from weak to strong. We started each one for you.

large huge big

→

big _____ _____

amazing great good

→

_____ _____ amazing

happy joyful glad

→

_____ happy _____

Make a Ten

Alex wants to make groups of **10** objects. Count and write the number of objects in each group. Then draw more objects so each group has 10 in all. Write the number of objects you drew to complete the equation.

☐ + ☐ = 10

☐ + ☐ = 10

☐ + ☐ = 10

To the Beat of 10

Count down from 10, stomping once for each number.

Each bar on this xylophone shows 2 numbers that add up to **10**. Complete an equation for each set of numbers. We did the first one to get you started.

Count up to 10, clapping once for each number.

$0 + 10 = 10$

$1 + \square = 10$

$2 + \square = 10$

$3 + \square = 10$

$4 + \square = 10$

$5 + \square = 10$

Lost Baby Bobcat

What other animals do you see?

Can you help Mama Bobcat find her kitten? Read the sentences about the picture. Trace and say each red word. Then write the word.

Does Mama Bobcat have a sad face?

face

Her kitten is lost.

lost

The kitten is near a rock.

rock

It wants to play with the caterpillar.

play

Mama Bobcat will soon find her kitten.

find

Yy

Trace and write uppercase Y and lowercase y.

Y y Y y

Trace this tongue twister. See if you can say it five times, fast!

Yes, Yolanda
Yak is yakking.

Copy these y words and say them aloud.

yo-yo

yarn

yolk

yellow

March On

It's the day of the big parade, and Pat's Party Place is selling lots of parade props! Solve the word problems below to help Pat figure out how many items she has left. We did the first one to get you started.

Pat had **9** drums. She sold **3** drums. How many drums are left?

$9 - 3 = 6$

Pat had **8** unicycles. She sold **1** unicycle. How many unicycles are left?

$\square - \square = \square$

Pat had **10** balloons. She sold **2** balloons. How many balloons are left?

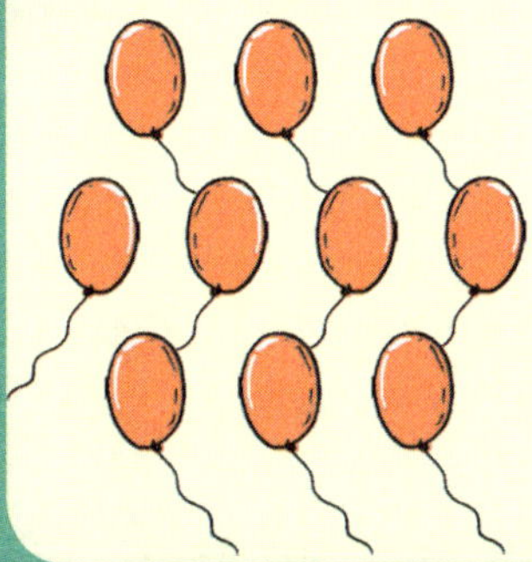

$\square - \square = \square$

Game On!

The arrow of each symbol points to the smaller number.

The Yellow Jackets baseball team played 12 games. Did they score more, less, or the same as each team they played?

Draw the symbol > (greater than), < (less than), or = (equal to) to complete each set of scores. We did the first one to get you started.

GAME 1	4	<	6
GAME 2	7		3
GAME 3	8		7
GAME 4	3		3
GAME 5	6		5
GAME 6	7		7
GAME 7	5		5
GAME 8	2		5
GAME 9	9		4
GAME 10	8		10
GAME 11	3		4
GAME 12	9		6

What did the glove say to the baseball?

"Catch you later!"

Circle the baseball with the number that makes the statement true. We did the first one to get you started.

4	>	3 (circled)	5	4
6	<	4	6	7
8	=	3	8	5
3	>	2	3	4
9	<	9	8	10

Zz

Trace and write uppercase **Z** and lowercase **z**.

Zz Zz

Trace this tongue twister. See if you can say it five times, fast!

Zoey zips
and zooms.

How many **Z**'s can you find in this picture?

Color in 3-D

Cubes, cylinders, and spheres are all 3-D shapes.

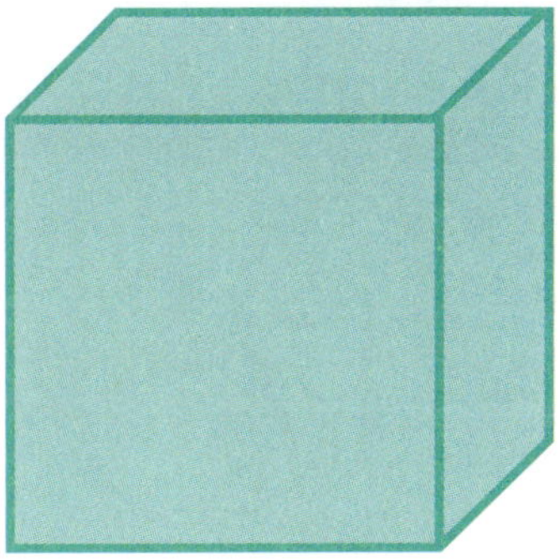

A cube has 6 sides.

A sphere is curved.

A cylinder has 2 flat ends and 1 curved side.

Color each cube blue. Color each cylinder red. Color each sphere yellow.

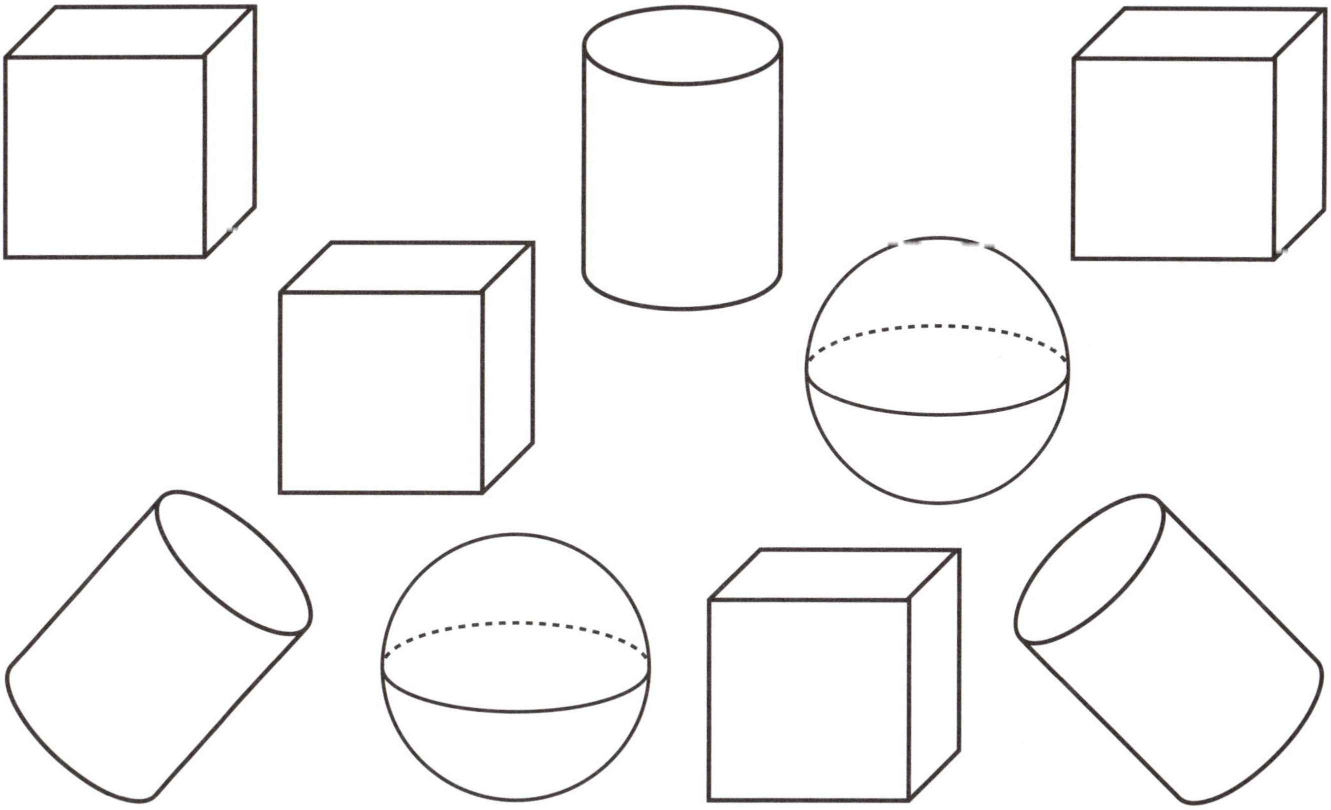

Let's Play Ball

Solve each addition problem. How many more sports balls do you need? Draw that many circles in the space below the problem. Then write the number to complete the equation.

$$10 + \square = 17$$

$$10 + \square = 18$$

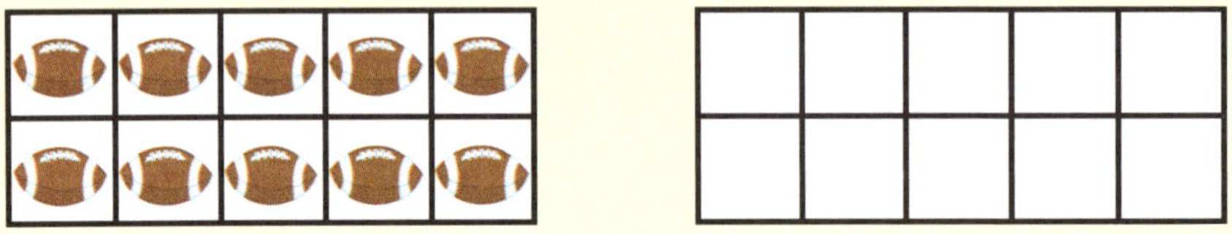

$$10 + \square = 19$$

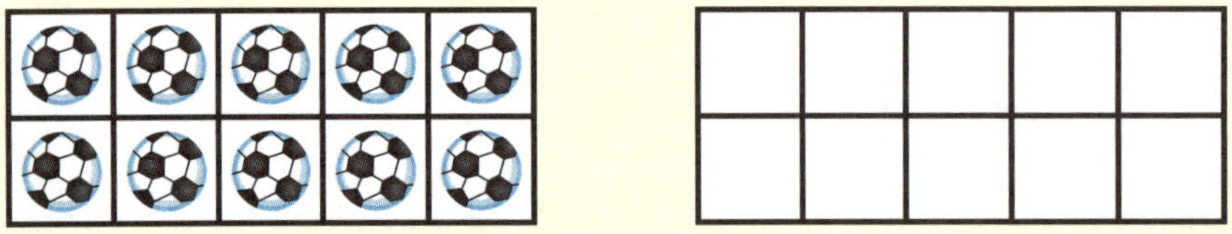

$19 = 10 + \square$

$18 = 10 + \square$

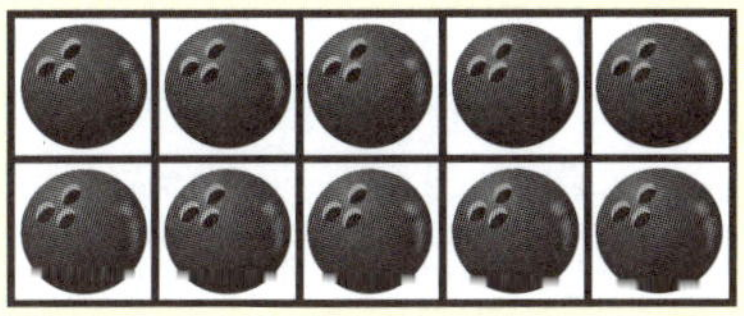

$17 = 10 + \square$

Clouds and Weather

Read the story and then answer the questions.

Clouds come in many shapes and sizes. Have you seen clouds that look like these?

Look at these feathery clouds. They are usually a sign of fair weather.

These white clouds are puffy. They can mean fair weather, too. But be careful if they get dark! That might mean rain.

These clouds are dark. A storm is probably on the way.

Look at the clouds when you are getting ready to go outside. They can help you decide if you need your umbrella!

Why is it a good idea to look at the clouds before you go outside?

Which kinds of clouds show that it might rain?

What kind of clouds would you hope to see at an outdoor picnic?

Time to Time

The little hand points to the hour. The big hand points to the minute.

Which clocks show the same time? Draw a line from each clock to its match.

Congratulations! You've completed **Chapter 8**—and this *Summer Big Fun Workbook*. **GREAT JOB!** Place your Chapter 8 sticker on your poster. Try this activity, then fill out your Achievement Certificate.

BONUS!
Summer Craft Activity

Rock On!

YOU WILL NEED:

- Smooth rocks
- Tempera paint
- Paintbrush
- Glue

What other materials can sculptures be made from?

1. With an adult's permission, find a place to work outside or cover a table with newspaper. Spread out the rocks. Paint the rocks and let them dry.

2. Arrange the rocks in a pleasing shape and glue them together to make a sculpture.

3. Place your sculpture in a special place as a decoration.

Answers

Page 11
It's Time to Rhyme!

Here are the rhymes we found. You might have found others.

1. fox in socks
2. baboon with a bassoon
3. sheep in a jeep
4. llamas in pajamas
5. frog on a log
6. tennis racket in a jacket
7. duck with a puck
8. cat with a bat
9. bear in a chair
10. goat in a coat
11. lizard who is a wizard
12. raccoon with a balloon
13. kittens wearing mittens
14. pug on a rug
15. lamp with a stamp
16. mouse with a blouse

Page 14
Cc

Page 16
Dd

Page 21
Fruit Addition

1 + 2 = 3

3 + 2 = 5

2 + 2 = 4

1 + 1 = 2

Page 25
10

Page 32
Gg

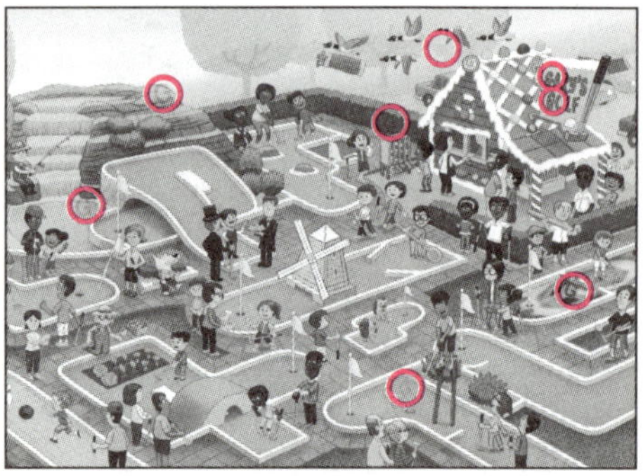

Page 22
Ee

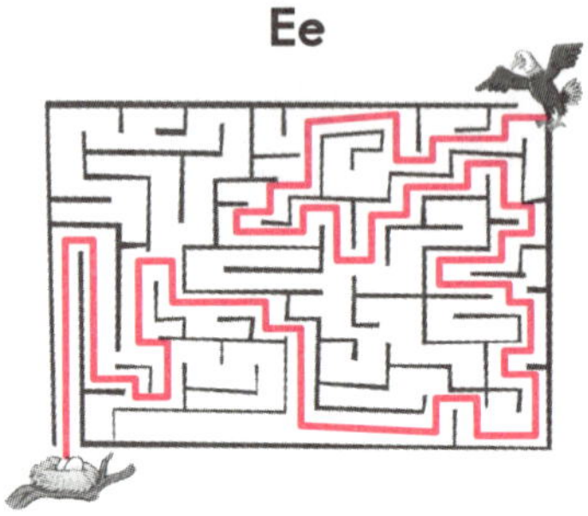

Page 33
Gumball Subtraction

2 − 1 = 1

3 − 1 = 2

5 − 2 = 3

4 − 3 = 1

Page 46
Kk

Page 52
Road Trip!

Page 38
Ii

Page 55
Mail Match

2 + 2 = 4	3 + 2 = 5
1 + 2 = 3	0 + 3 = 3
0 + 1 = 1	2 + 0 = 2
1 + 1 = 2	3 + 1 = 4
4 + 1 = 5	1 + 0 = 1

Answers

Pages 62–63
On the Farm

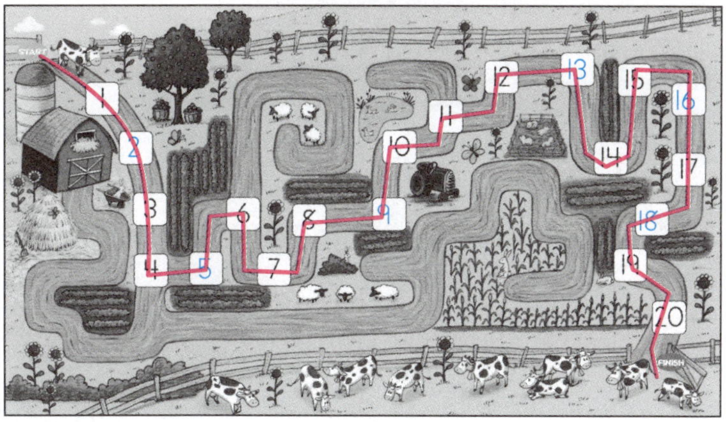

There are more sheep than pigs.

Page 64
Oo

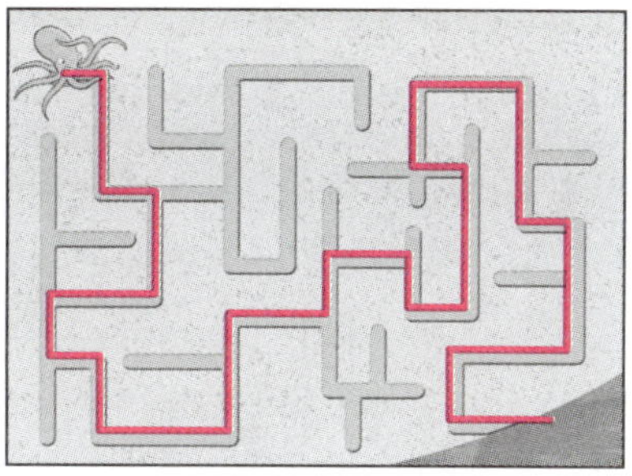

Page 67
Penny Addition

2 + 4 = 6
4 + 6 = 10
5 + 3 = 8
6 + 3 = 9

Pages 68–69
Finding a Home

Why does a hermit crab need a shell?
To stay safe.

How does a hermit crab get a new shell?
It must find an empty shell that will be just right.

Why is the size of a shell important to a hermit crab?
So the crab can escape danger and easily carry its new home.

Page 74
Qq

Page 75
Number Quilt

Page 76
Playground Cats

Page 82
Ss

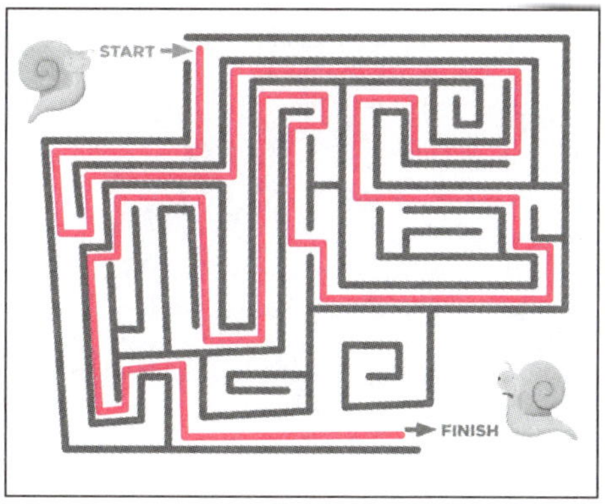

Page 84
Which Word?

Anna swims in the big pool.

The girls catch the water balloons.

Eli hops over the short fence.

The bunnies hop on the grass.

Mom and I swim in the ocean.

The puppy catches the ball.

Page 79
Fact Family Rocket

2 + 3 = 5
5 − 3 = 2
3 + 2 = 5
5 − 2 = 3

Page 83
Sheep Subtraction

9 − 2 = 7
9 − 1 = 8
7 − 1 = 6
10 − 4 = 6

Answers

Page 85
Which Word?

Which word means to become less strong?
weakest — **weaken** (circled)

Which word means someone who finishes last in a group?
slower — **slowest** (circled)

Which word means to take a lot of care?
careful (circled) — careless

Which word means to make something hot again?
preheat — **reheat** (circled)

Which word means the door is not bolted?
unlocked (circled) — relocked

Page 86
Who Uses What?

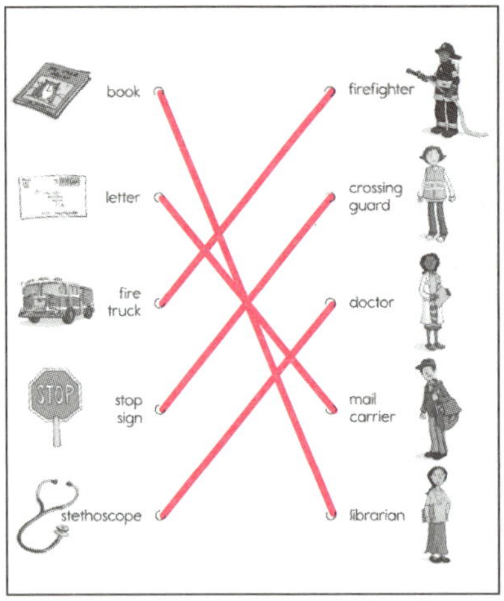

Pages 90–91
Tiny Creatures

10 + 1 = 11
10 + 2 = 12
10 + 3 = 13

13 = 10 + 3
12 = 10 + 2
11 = 10 + 1

Page 94
Here We Go!

Page 98
Under the Ocean

2 + 1 = 3 1 + 4 = 5

Page 99
Umbrellas for Sale

3 − 3 = 0 4 − 2 = 2

BONUS PROBLEM: She has 1 dollar left.

Pages 102–103
Bang! Clang! Big Dump Truck!

What sounds does the truck make?
Bang! Clang! Beep, beep, beep.

Who is watching the dump truck?
The kids and their dad.

Where does this story take place? How do you know?
You can see the work takes place on the city streets by the illustrations.

Page 101
Vacation Time

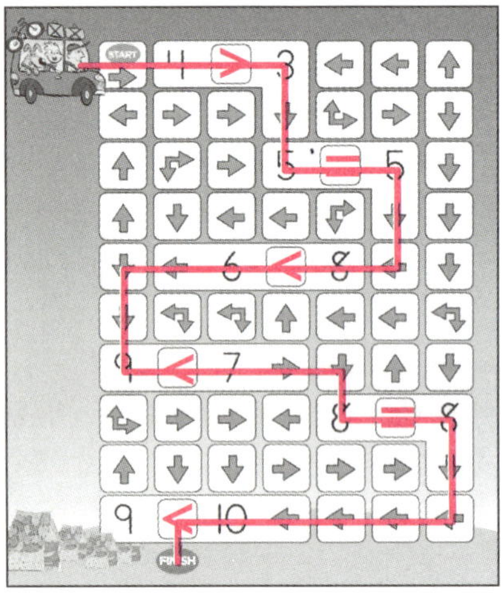

Pages 106–107
Space Travel

Object	Tally
	卌 |||
	卌 |
	||||

Page 113
The Big Roundup

6 + 4 = 10 4 + 5 = 9

BONUS: The pen with sheep has the most animals in it.

Page 108
In the Woods

Pages 110–111
Fact Family Flip Flops

6 + 4 = 10
10 − 6 = 4

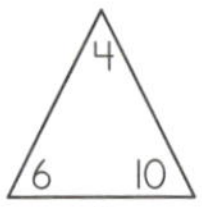

4 + 6 = 10
10 − 4 = 6

5 + 3 = 8
8 − 3 = 5

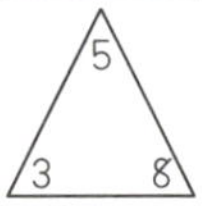

3 + 5 = 8
8 − 5 = 3

2 + 4 = 6
6 − 2 = 4

4 + 2 = 6
6 − 4 = 2

7 + 2 = 9
9 − 2 = 7

2 + 7 = 9
9 − 7 = 2

Page 114
What's It Like?

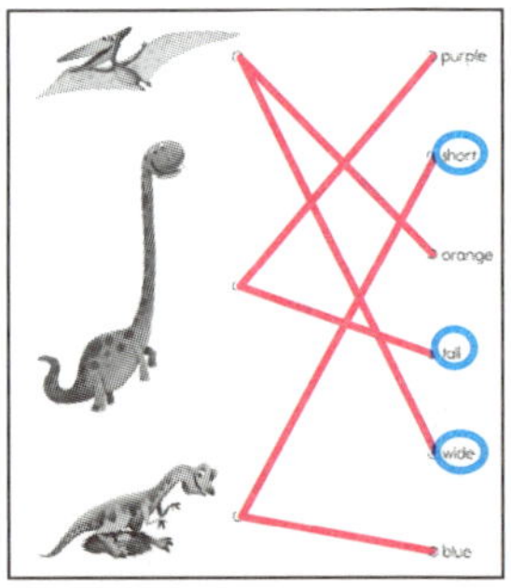

Answers

Page 117
Grid Maze

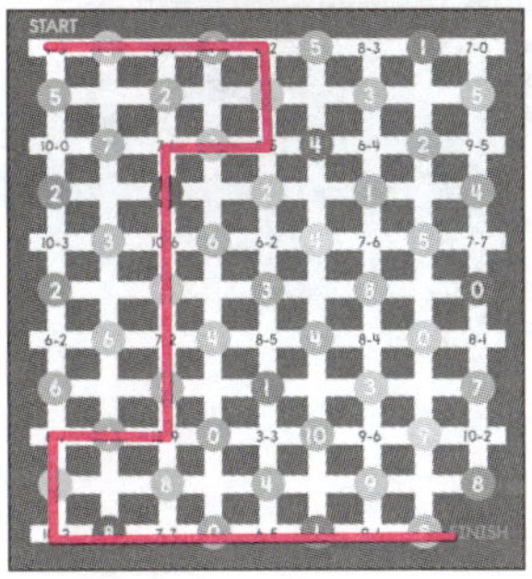

Pages 118–119
Just Add Food!

10 + 4 = 14

10 + 5 = 15

10 + 6 = 16

16 = 10 + 6

15 = 10 + 5

14 = 10 + 4

Page 123
Strong Words

big → large → huge

good → great → amazing

glad → happy → joyful

Page 124
Make a Ten

8 + 2 = 10

6 + 4 = 10

7 + 3 = 10

Page 125
To the Beat of 10

1 + 9 = 10

2 + 8 = 10

3 + 7 = 10

4 + 6 = 10

5 + 5 = 10

Page 129
March On

8 − 1 = 7

10 − 2 = 8

Pages 130–131
Game On!

GAME 1	4	<	6	GAME 7	5	=	5
GAME 2	7	>	3	GAME 8	2	<	5
GAME 3	8	>	7	GAME 9	9	>	4
GAME 4	3	=	3	GAME 10	8	<	10
GAME 5	6	>	5	GAME 11	3	<	4
GAME 6	7	=	7	GAME 12	9	>	6

4	>	(3)	5	4
6	<	4	6	(7)
8	=	3	(8)	5
3	>	(2)	3	4
9	<	9	8	(10)

Page 132
Zz

Pages 136–137
Clouds and Weather

Why is it a good idea to look at the clouds before you go outside?
They can help you decide if you need your umbrella!

Which kinds of clouds show that it might rain?
Dark clouds.

What kind of clouds would you hope to see at an outdoor picnic?
Feathery and white, puffy clouds are a sign of good weather.

Pages 134–135
Let's Play Ball

10 + 7 = 17

10 + 8 = 18

10 + 9 = 19

19 = 10 + 9

18 = 10 + 8

17 = 10 + 7

Page 138
Time to Time

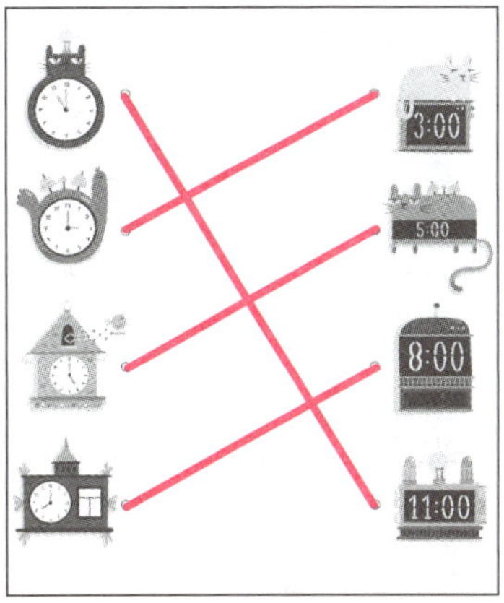

Summer Big Fun Adventure Progress Poster

Highlights™

BRIDGING GRADES K&1

Congratulations!

(your name)

worked hard
and finished the

Summer
Big Fun Workbook

Summer Stickers

BRIDGING GRADES K&1

When you finish a chapter, place that chapter's sticker on the matching sign on the poster. Finish all 8 chapters and place all 8 stickers to complete your **Summer Big Fun Adventure**!

Use these sun stickers to mark each spot on the poster where you find a hidden seashell.

Place these emoji stickers on your favorite pages in this book—or use them to decorate a notebook or share with friends!